The Cambridge Introduction to
Jean Rhys

Since her death in 1979, Jean Rhys's reputation as an important modernist author has grown. Her finely crafted prose fiction lends itself to multiple interpretations from radically different critical perspectives, formalism, feminism, and postcolonial studies along them. This Introduction offers a reliable and stimulating account of her life, work, contexts and critical reception. Her best-known novel, *Wide Sargasso Sea*, is analyzed together with her other novels, including *Quartet* and *After Leaving Mr Mackenzie*, and her short stories. Through close readings of the works, Elaine Savory reveals their common themes and connects these to different critical approaches. The book maps Rhys's fictional use of the actual geography of Paris, London and the Caribbean, showing how key understanding her relationships with the metropolitan and colonial spheres is to reading her texts. In this invaluable introduction for students and faculty, Savory explains the significance of Rhys as a writer both in her lifetime and today.

Elaine Savory is Associate Professor of English at the New School University. Her publications include *Jean Rhys* (Cambridge, 1998), *Out of the Kumbla: Women and Caribbean Literature* (1990) and many essays on Caribbean and African literatures.

The Cambridge Introduction to
Jean Rhys

ELAINE SAVORY
The New School University, New York City

CAMBRIDGE UNIVERSITY PRESS
Cambridge, New York, Melbourne, Madrid, Cape Town, Singapore, São Paulo, Delhi

Cambridge University Press
The Edinburgh Building, Cambridge CB2 8RU, UK

Published in the United States of America by Cambridge University Press, New York

www.cambridge.org
Information on this title: www.cambridge.org/9780521695435

First published 2009

Printed in the United Kingdom at the University Press, Cambridge

A catalogue record for this publication is available from the British Library

ISBN 978-0-521-87366-6 hardback
ISBN 978-0-521-69543-5 paperback

For Stacy, 1963–2008

Mais elle était du monde, où les plus belles choses
Ont le pire destin,
Et rose elle a vécu ce que vivent les roses,
L'espace d'un matin.

François de Malherbe

Contents

Preface

This story begins with a powerful literary lion, Ford Madox Ford, loving and mentoring a beautiful, much younger, very gifted woman in the heady literary atmosphere of 1920s Paris. The connection between them did not last but the woman became the writer Jean Rhys. Her literary style was immediately highly praised but, after a collection of short stories and four novels, she sank into obscurity for almost three decades. Then her fifth and last novel catapulted her into literary stardom in her middle seventies. Her timing was perfect. This exquisitely crafted text appealed to readers interested in the exploitation of women, in race and in colonialism, all important issues in the mid-1960s, a time when West Indian immigration to Britain also brought the Caribbean more into the consciousness of the reading public.

It was gradually discovered that the life of the woman behind the writer was also a gripping story. The given name of Jean Rhys was Ella Gwendoline Rees Williams. She was from an elite family in the colonial Caribbean. She went to England to find her future, became an unsuccessful chorus girl, suffered the death of her father, and almost immediately afterwards, she got her heart broken by a rich gentleman and subsequently fell into a period of rackety living before her first marriage. She had strained relationships with most of her original family. Her first child died as a young baby, and she was separated from her second child for long periods of time. She had three husbands, two of whom went to jail for petty fraud, while the other was an unsuccessful literary agent. Neither they nor she were much good at sustaining a steady income, so her life was very often a struggle for basic shelter and daily necessities. She gradually became a serious alcoholic and in middle age was arrested for disturbing the peace and was briefly confined in a women's prison for psychiatric evaluation. Many assumed she had died when she disappeared from public view for decades, so when she reappeared, there was talk of a "reincarnation." She thought neighbours in her village in Devon imagined her a witch, which she enjoyed. Her refusal to give in or give up finally gave her an aura, as if she were capable of magical transformations and reincarnations and possessed mysterious powers. She did nothing to dispel this idea.

But the life story can mislead the new reader of Rhys. She lied about her age and fooled her early critics if they failed to think carefully about the timeline of her life. Then the unwary reader may be lured into thinking her protagonists are Rhys herself, and that there is really therefore only one "Rhys woman," recycled through different texts. But Rhys's texts ask her readers to absent themselves from the novel's frequent affiliation with unexamined middle-class values and prejudices and live in her much less comfortable fictional world. She challenges us to take nothing for granted and to read her closely.

She lived long (1890–1979), and it is less than forty years since she died, a literary blink of the eye. Separating the life story from the literary achievement is easier as time goes on: it has been nearly seventy years since James Joyce, Rhys's rough contemporary (1882–1941), died prematurely. T. S. Eliot (1888–1965) was only two years older than Rhys, and lived to his late seventies, but he sternly ordered his readers to forget about his personality when reading his work. Significant writers offer clues as to how to read their work and need their readership to learn their writing games. But the problem with Rhys was that she was far ahead of her time. When her early work appeared, some people thought she was thirty or forty years ahead, which would have made her moment the mid-1960s, when her greatest success happened. But she is coming into full focus now for a new generation, in a new century. Whilst the readings of Rhys's work so popular at the height of the feminist movement can be insightful, neither they nor other one-dimensional readings of her work (such as modernist-aesthetic or postcolonial) do justice to her texts by themselves. As we realize more multifaceted ways of reading her, we also ask ourselves to be conscious that our own responses to the world are complicated and changing. So, despite periodic predictions that her meteoric rise to fame must inevitably be followed by a fall in her reputation, she continues to fascinate those who enter her fictional world.

The new reader will therefore benefit from a guide to Rhys. This introduction to her work offers a map that is both extensive and detailed. Chapter 1 sorts out biographical fact from fiction, Chapter 2 locates her work in important contexts that help us become more savvy readers of her work and Chapter 4 explores important trends in Rhys criticism. But the longest chapter here is a close reading of Rhys's published texts, which demonstrates her consummate skill at crafting fiction. Her texts, whilst telling stories located in particular times and places and imaginatively drawing on her own experience, are nevertheless timeless, something she deliberately sought to achieve.

There is a short booklist of useful further reading (for a discussion of Rhys criticism broader than this book can allow, see my *Jean Rhys* (1998, 2000, 2001, 2006). My purpose here is to share my own pleasure in reading Jean Rhys, a pleasure sharpened by knowing the work of many fine scholars and critics who have also found her irresistible. She is a writer of many identities and aspects. This is my second book on Rhys and it has taken me along different paths from the first, because Rhys's work is rich and subtle enough to offer new experiences in successive readings, a clear sign of the quality of her work. I wish you the joy of discovering this unusual and finely developed literary talent for yourself.

Acknowledgments

First and foremost, I thank Ray Ryan, who is the most productively and insightfully impatient of patient editors. He initiated the idea of this project when I thought I was done with Rhys. He has also been there for me during the personally difficult time of its completion.

My first book on Rhys (Cambridge, 1998) brought me the world of Rhys scholarship, and my thanks to all who assisted me then remain even now. I thank my students at Eugene Lang College, New School University, over a number of years, for their willingness to become better readers of Rhys (as of other texts), and my colleagues at NSU, who are always supportive. For Rhys scholars and Caribbean writers she is always a key topic, even when they are done with writing about her: they smile when I say I am haunted by Mis' Rhys, because they are too.

Thanks are due to the Rhys Collection at the University of Tulsa for permission to quote from unpublished manuscripts.

This book had to be completed during our beloved Stacy's long and hard-fought battle against ultimately terminal illness, and so has been by far the most difficult project I have ever had. To Austin and Todd, my thanks for accepting what your extraordinary sister also was very clear about, that a task undertaken has to become a task completed, however challenging it proves to be. To my love, Robert, thank you as always, for everything, especially in this most wounding of times.

Abbreviations

These editions of Rhys texts are referenced. Their titles in the references are abbreviated as follows:

ALMM	*After Leaving Mr. Mackenzie* (first published 1931), New York: Carroll and Graf, 1990.
CS	*The Collected Short Stories* (includes all of Rhys's three story collections, *The Left Bank* (London: Jonathan Cape, 1927), *Tigers Are Better-Looking* (London: André Deutsch, 1968) and *Sleep It Off Lady* (London: André Deutsch, 1976). These three titles are abbreviated as *TLB*, *TABL* and *SIOL* respectively.
GMM	*Good Morning, Midnight* (first published 1939), New York: W. W. Norton, 1986.
L	*The Letters of Jean Rhys* (edited by Francis Wyndham and Diana Athill), New York: Viking Penguin, 1984.
Q	*Quartet* (first published 1929), New York: Carroll and Graf, 1990.
SP	*Smile Please: An Unfinished Autobiography*, Berkeley: Donald S. Ellis, 1979.
V	*Voyage in the Dark* (first published 1934), New York: W. W. Norton, 1982.
WSS	*Wide Sargasso Sea* (first published 1966), New York: W. W. Norton, 1982.

Chapter 1

Life

Jean Rhys was a pen name, for a woman who thought the only important aspects of a writer are in the work. But her biography is important, precisely because she was often vague about key aspects of it, and therefore knowing her life as accurately as possible gives us valuable insights into how she worked the raw material of experience into fiction.

Gwen Williams 1890–1907

There is first the matter of name, something that reverberates in Rhys's work. She was christened Ella Gwendoline Rees Williams, and later (on the stage or in married life) was known as Ella, Vivien or Emma Grey, Ella Lenglet or Ella Hamer. Gwendolen is the spelling on her tombstone, and the one she used in her autobiography, *Smile Please.* But she was christened Gwendoline.[1] She hated the name Gwendolen (which she learned means white in Welsh), just as she hated being the palest of her siblings (five in all surviving): they had brown eyes and hair, and she had blue eyes, fair skin and lighter hair (*SP*:14).

Dominica, where she was born, on August 24, 1890, is still a wildly beautiful island, the heavily forested, mostly undeveloped top of a submerged volcano which still produces the sulfurous "Boiling Lake" in its crater.[2] In her childhood, it was very difficult to get around, and boats were often used to go from one part of the island to another. Hesketh Bell, the famous colonial

Administrator of Dominica (1899–1905), tried to build the "Imperial Road" to facilitate colonial plantations on the island: it was never finished.[3]

Dominica was a colony of Britain with a long history of slavery and a white English hegemony. But, unusually in the Caribbean at the time, this was challenged by a powerful, mixed-race elite, whose slave-owning ancestors had migrated from Saint Domingue around 1790.[4] In 1838, they were known as the "Mulatto Ascendancy" when they became the majority in the House of Assembly. They held onto this power until Crown Colony Rule was imposed by the British to obtain more direct colonial control in 1898.[5] The Lockharts, Gwen Williams' mother's white Creole family, belonged to the Anglican, British faction, established prominently in Dominica for five generations by the time of Rhys's birth, since James Potter Lockhart emigrated to Dominica to first manage a sugar plantation, Geneva, and then by the mid-1820s to own it, along with 258 slaves.[6] He became a powerful political figure in Dominica. His wife Jean was reputedly a Spanish princess from Cuba, though the young Gwen did not believe this story (*SP*:26). She was perhaps of mixed race, not uncommon among Creoles, but an issue for Rhys's mother's family, who liked to think their bloodline was only English.[7]

Gwen Williams was eight when the English made Dominica a Crown Colony. Property qualifications for voting were very high in Dominica at the time, so few could vote, but elected representation was prized and defended. Crown Colony rule replaced elected representatives with a Legislative Council made up of six officials and six members nominated by the Administrator.[8] Jean Rhys still remembered in old age how Administrator Hesketh Bell (known for charming those who were still angry about the political change) gave a very enjoyable fancy-dress ball for children in honor of his niece and paid her special attention (*SP*:73–4).[9] In that period, a thriving newspaper rivalry expressed the competing interests of the colonial English and brown skin elite, demonstrating the power and value of verbal skills: that she knew about this is clear in her short story, "Again the Antilles" (*CS*:39–41).[10]

Rhys's Welsh father, William Rees Williams, ran off to sea at fourteen and was quickly taken home, but eventually joined the Merchant Navy. He later completed medical school.[11] One of the feisty local papers, *The Dominica Dial*, reported that his medical career had begun inauspiciously on board a ship repairing telegraph communications, but his luck changed when he got a colonial appointment as a doctor in Roseau, Dominica's capital. He later temporarily acquired two estates in the interior of Dominica to which the family went via coastal steamer and horseback. The larger one Rhys remembered was called Bona Vista (*SP*:15) It had a wide and impressive view of Dominica's forested Mornes (the term for mountains in Dominica as in the French Caribbean), but also across valleys to the sea. In "Mixing

Cocktails," Rhys recalls the view from "the house in the hills" (*CS*:36–7). Though the house has all but vanished, the site affirms the spectacular view. In Roseau, the family lived in a pleasant, colonial-style house not far from the waterfront, with a jalousied balcony overlooking the main street and a courtyard at the back. It was here that Dr. Williams had his practice.[12] The opening of Rhys's third novel (*Voyage in the Dark*) describes looking down a street from "the house at home" to "the Bay": standing in front of Rhys's family home in Roseau, this is the view down to the sea.

The majority of Dominica's population are of African descent, mainly speaking French Creole and of the Catholic faith. Slavery ended there earlier than in neighbouring Guadaloupe and Martinique, from where slaves then fled to Dominica.[13] Race and shade permeated Rhys's child consciousness. When given a fair doll (her sister got the dark-haired one she wanted), she took it into the garden and ritually smashed its face with a rock (*SP*:30–1). She had a dark-skinned nurse, Meta, who, by Rhys's account, often played on her child's credulity, and told her terrifying stories of spirits and demons. She had to witness the annual Carnival procession from within her house, since it was an expression of the black Dominican community, though she was sent out with money to give to the stilt-man called the Bois-Bois. She had a close friendship "with a Negro girl called Francine" (*SP*:23) who was a very good storyteller. The Anglican church in Roseau, where the Williams family worshipped along with others willing to be affiliated with Britain, had segregated seats and entrances: whites sat at the front with a space between them and black congregants, who were fewer in number. Rhys remembered not having any problems with this arrangement as a child (*SP*:72), and reported yelling "Black Devil" at Meta. She had both what Ford Madox Ford called her "passion for stating the case of the underdog"[14] and a capacity to sound thoroughly white English colonial: "I never tried to be friends with any of the colored girls again . . . They hate us. We are hated" (*SP*:39). Rhys was contradictory about race. She was romantic about black culture as a child (she thought it more fun than white), but in old age she could sound resentful at the loss of white power in Dominica.

Race and colonialism figure in two stories about Gwen Williams' adolescent life, one a highly suspect rumor and the other recorded in one of Rhys's writing notebooks. The rumor is that Rhys might have had a love interest in someone partly Carib (this is based on a piece of fiction which her brother Owen wrote).[15] It seems, however, unlikely that such a violation of racial mores could have gone unnoticed in a world where adolescent white girls were constantly under supervision and servants noticed everything. But there is a sense of forbidden love across racial caste lines in the submerged story of Sandi and Antoinette in *Wide Sargasso Sea* (1966). Then, in the

Black Exercise Book, Rhys wrote an account of being sexually and psychologically abused by an old Englishman, Mr. Howard, who touched her breast once, and then developed a sadomasochistic serial story about her sexual submission to him.[16] The married Howard was an emblem of colonial English privilege. Rhys's mother, thinking him a charming old gentleman, sent her daughter out with him to the Botanical Gardens in Roseau. Thus Rhys did not dare to tell her mother. The incident could easily have been amongst those aspects of her life that Rhys erased. But though she only wrote of it clearly in one story, she never lost her notebook account of it (and she lost much else). The narrative of a young female victim of sexual abuse is clearly one source of the sexual inhibition or emotional masochism that most of Rhys's protagonists display. Another is the devastating end of her first serious love affair.

Gwen Williams and Ella Gray 1907–1919

Gwen Williams left Dominica to complete her education under the guardianship of her English aunt, Clarice.[17] In Roseau, she had attended a convent school as a boarder, and in England she would again be a boarder at the Perse School for Girls in Cambridge, leaving in 1908. In 1909 she enrolled at what would become the Royal Academy of Dramatic Art (then called, after its founder Beerbohm Tree, Tree's School). She left the same year and defied her family's wishes to go on the stage as a chorus girl, choosing Ella Gray (or sometimes, Vivien or Emma Gray) as her stage name. Though Rhys said she left Tree's School because her father died, Angier points out that he died in 1910, and that the real reason was that her West Indian accent was not acceptable for serious theater in England at the time (*SP*:86–91).[18]

Rhys writes about her chorus-girl experience in her autobiography (*SP*:86–91). The life she lived was both gloriously fake (makeup, costumes and make-believe during the performances), and brutally real (tawdry boarding houses in which the chorus spent their leisure time). In old age, Rhys was often seen as an elderly siren, always made up and responsive to male attention: this was the way she had learned to face the public as a shy young woman. Chorus girls were also very often working class, and took part in the pub culture of Britain. This may have been where Rhys first began to drink: there may have been a tendency to alcoholism in her family, because her father was described in the Dominican press as being too fond of the bottle. Chorus girls were also prey for men of means. Lancelot Grey Hugh Smith took up with Rhys, but she fell very much in love. He was well to do, single, well connected, a successful stockbroker by profession at a time when that was breaking ground, and he had a London town house and a significant family home in the country. He was also twenty years older. Their relationship followed the usual pattern of such a man's casual sexual arrangements. He saw her when he felt like it, took her out to dinner, gave her money, had her visit him at his grand London town house but sent her home in a taxi before dawn, and was usually away at the weekends seeing his own family and friends at his parents' country house.[19] The relationship with Smith was in a sense a stage set, a place where the young Rhys could taste an English life she would have enjoyed, and forget that it was not anchored in real life.

Smith ended the affair before it got too serious for, whatever Rhys thought and hoped about her suitability for him, he would never have considered a white Creole chorus girl a likely long-term partner (moreover he never found any satisfactory candidate and remained unmarried). Following the social custom for men who indulged in cross-class affairs but wanted to be gentlemanly, he arranged for her to be financially supported, through money sent by his lawyer, for a number of years. But Rhys was emotionally devastated. Many years later she reflected: "It seems to me now that the whole business of money and sex is mixed up with something primitive and deep. When you take money directly from somebody you love it becomes not money but a symbol" (*SP*:97). Money and sex are often deeply intertwined in her fiction.

Her emotional collapse at the end of the affair is presented in her autobiography as triggering her entry into obsessively writing a journal, experienced as an extraordinary event: "My fingers tingled, and the palms of my hands . . . I wrote on until late into the night . . ." (*SP*:104). Writing thus became a release – but her portrayal of this as having the force of a conversion is likely a fiction, having the sort of shape actual experience would not: Diana Athill, Rhys's devoted editor for *Wide Sargasso Sea*, remarks that Rhys felt she had to rework experience to fit "the shape and nature of the work of art."[20]

Rhys's admission in her autobiography that she had an abortion ("after what was then called an illegal operation," *SP*:95) is located just after her lover leaves for New York (the end of the affair). It is followed by a suicidal period, and then the release into writing. Angier feels the timeline is the end of the affair in 1912, and the drift into a risky demi-monde life in 1913, including pregnancy and abortion early in that year.[21] She locates a particular intensity in Rhys's habit of writing notebooks from late 1913 into early 1914: these would become key sources for her fiction.

Rhys had a good many friends in the arts, suggesting that, though she loved a man who was in finance, she already wanted to spend a lot of time with artists early on, whether on the stage or not. However, she wrote sparingly about this. In *Smile Please*, Rhys speaks of a journalist called Alan, a proposal of marriage from someone she meets in a nightclub in 1914, a job in a crowd scene in a play, volunteering during the war in a canteen serving soldiers leaving for France, and a Belgian refugee called Camille whom she meets in a house in Torrington Square. Angier locates these men and others during the period between the affair with Smith and Rhys's first marriage: society painter Sir Edward Poynter (for whom Rhys posed), Alan Bott (subeditor on the *Daily Chronicle*, a leading national paper), Maxwell Henry Hayes Macartney (a journalist with *The Times*, to whom Rhys was engaged for a while), Adrian Allinson (a painter), Arthur Henry Fox Strangways (music critic for *The Times*) and Philip Heseltine (a composer and music critic).[22] Rhys's story "Till September Petronella" reflects this period, particularly through two artistic male characters, the music critic Julian and the artist Marston (*CS*).

Jean Rhys and Ella Lenglet 1919–1927

In 1919, Rhys had the pleasure of writing to her former lover, Smith, and telling him that his lawyer could stop sending her cheques (*SP*:113) because she was going to marry Willem Johan Marie (Jean) Lenglet. The marriage took place in The Hague on April 30. Angier offers details of how complicated this relationship really was, given that Lenglet was still, presumably unbeknown to Rhys, married to Marie Pollart until 1925. He left Rhys in Paris for periods during 1922–4. But Angier's portrait is not nearly as sympathetic and interesting as that of Kappers-den Hollander, who gives much more evidence of his complexity.[23] He was evidently a fine linguist, a brave soldier in World War I and a fighter against injustice who took enormous personal risks to combat fascism. He was entirely careless about paperwork, though he engaged in currency and art dealings, but this needs to be contextualized by the chaos of war and the aftermath of war. Many who profited far more deliberately got away with it. He was eventually a fugitive and a stateless person, arrested in 1924, accused of fraud and jailed. The Lenglets had two children, the first a boy, William Owen, who died in infancy in early 1920, and the second a girl, Maryvonne, born in May 1922, when Rhys and her husband could not afford to keep a child, so that Maryvonne probably spent some time in a clinic or with Rhys's friends.[24]

Rhys was highly protective of her daughter, and the experience of motherhood is almost entirely erased from her fiction. During the difficult period of Lenglet's absences, Rhys may have stayed with H. Pearl Adam, a journalist and the wife of a journalist, who later, when Rhys tried to sell her translations of some of Lenglet's work, encouraged her to develop her diaries into fiction, and even edited them herself into the never-published novel "Triple Sec." It was Mrs. Adams who, via this manuscript, introduced Rhys to Ford Madox Ford.

Ford was a literary impresario and indefatigable if uneven writer (he published eighty-one books and over four hundred articles).[25] He was known for helping and publishing promising writers, including D. H. Lawrence, Graham Greene and Wyndham Lewis. He held court in Paris restaurants, most famously Le Dôme, and made temporary consecutive sexual connections with attractive and gifted young female writers to boost his creative energies. Rhys moved in for a while with Ford and his companion of the previous six years, painter Stella Bowen, who eventually described Rhys as having a "needle-quick intelligence and a good sort of honesty" but also called her a "doomed soul, violent and demoralized."[26] Ford's affair with Rhys did serious damage to his relationship with Bowen, but for Rhys it was a very helpful training ground for her future work.[27]

She also had a strong friendship with Germaine Richelot, a kind, well-to-do and highly cultivated Jewish woman for whose family Rhys worked as a tutor for several months during her pregnancy with her first child, and who seems likely to have helped her a great deal. Also Rhys may have posed for a Jewish sculptor from England, Violet Dreschfeld.[28] There are minor but intriguing references to Jewish people and cultural symbols in her fiction: it seems likely that, over and above her loyalty to Jewish friends whom she loved, she also felt something of common cause between her own colonial displacement and the marginalization of Jews in Europe during the 1920s and 1930s.

No doubt being in Paris helped her remember the French Creole that so flourished in Dominica in her childhood. She developed a strong love for French poetry. She began to earn money by work related to writing quite early. During the ending of her affair with Ford, she worked briefly for a Mrs. Hudnut, a rich American woman with writing ambitions who lived in the South of France. She also translated a novel, *Perversité*, by Francis Carco, though when it appeared Ford's name was on the title page.[29] Lenglet and Rhys communicated in French and, in this period of her life, constant translation between French and English must have sharpened her sense of each word she used, as did her lifelong love of poetry. In her papers, when she died, were poems she particularly enjoyed which she had copied out by hand. Her fiction has many of the attributes of the heightened, layered language of poetry.

Her first book was a volume of short stories, *The Left Bank* (1927). Ford published what became the last story in the collection, "Vienne," in his *transatlantic review*, which put this unknown and inexperienced writer in the company of modernist stars like Joyce, Hemingway, Pound, Djuna Barnes and Gertrude Stein, among others. He also helped her place the collection and wrote an introduction to the stories which is as much about him as about the stories, and has a patronizing tone at times, but was also important to Rhys's collection being noticed.

Jean Rhys 1928–1945

Rhys's second book was a novel, *Quartet* (1928), in which she fictionalized the affair with Ford. By the time it came out she was in London, now the writer, Jean Rhys. Rhys is a different spelling of her father's family name of Rees, and Jean could have been chosen for her husband, Jean, or her "Cuban" ancestor Jean, or both.

Quartet was only one of the four books that represented the "*affaire* Ford," the others being Jean Lenglet's novel, *Sous les Verrous* (written under the name Edouard de Nève, 1933), Ford's novel *When the Wicked Man* (1931), and Stella Bowen's account in her autobiography, *Drawn from Life* (1941). Rhys's fictional portrayal of Ford irritated him (and his friends among the London *literati*). He then wrote what is probably his worst novel, with a lurid white Creole character called Lola Porter who is suspected of murdering her husband and loves telling stories about voodoo and "obi" (obeah). Ford's narrator uncritically reflects the cultural and racial prejudices commonplace in Britain at the time, describing "Mrs Porter" in Harlem as insisting "on dancing half-naked in a regular tohuwabohu of negroes, mulatresses and gangsters."[30] Because Lenglet's novel was translated and edited by Rhys as *Barred*, appearing in Britain a year before his own version in French, we might see it as a fifth "version," by both of them.

When *Quartet* appeared, Rhys was living in London with Leslie Tilden Smith, a rather unsuccessful literary agent, who was very supportive of her work. It is ironical that she had romantic relationships with two Englishmen called L. Smith (Lancelot and Leslie). She married Tilden Smith on February 19, 1934 (the year *Voyage in the Dark* was published). Smith's daughter reported that he wrote to Ford to ask if he needed an English agent, and got the reply that Ford didn't but Rhys did. Ford sent Smith some of her stories, and Angier believes Smith was both domestically and professionally an important part of the literary productivity Rhys achieved between 1928 and 1939.[31] But Rhys strongly disliked London and England, and probably returned to Paris when she could. She and Lenglet divorced in 1928 (though their literary connection lasted longer and was complicated: over a number of years they each revised, built on, translated, or, in Lenglet's case, perhaps appropriated the other's work).[32] She helped *Barred* be published and reviewed in Britain. This is interesting proof that Rhys's strongest connections were those through writing: it was what she and both her first and second husbands really had in common.

After 1924, when the Lenglets separated, the plan was for their daughter Maryvonne to live with each parent as convenient. Though Maryvonne spent more time with her father as time went on, she did remember staying with her mother for six months in the South of France.[33] She was schooled in Amsterdam and visited her mother for holidays, thus relieving Rhys of the distraction of raising a child. Rhys was unable to be a normally domesticated wife and mother, though she clearly deeply loved her daughter.

She was thus able to commit herself to writing, and she really did, publishing her second novel, *After Leaving Mr. Mackenzie*, in 1931, her third, *Voyage in the Dark*, in 1934, and her fourth, *Good Morning, Midnight*, in 1939. She worked on shorter pieces of fiction. She had friendships with women who loved literature or wrote it (Peggy Kirkaldy and Evelyn Scott; see *L*). Scott, who liked *After Leaving Mr. Mackenzie*, shared something of Rhys's racial complexities, being white from a culture that had been built on racialized plantation slavery. She extended Rhys's knowledge of American literature. Their friendship was to founder, as did many of Rhys's connections with literary women (*L*:34).

In 1936, as a result of a bequest Leslie Tilden Smith received, Rhys was able to visit Dominica, the only time she saw it after she left as a teenager. This was crucial in giving her a vivid new set of memories of its topography and in refreshing childhood recollections. It was in New York on the way home from this trip that Rhys quarreled with Evelyn Scott.

The end of the thirties saw the onset of fascism in Germany and the start of World War II in 1939. This was the year Rhys's fourth novel, *Good Morning, Midnight* appeared: understandably it was largely ignored. She burned an early version of *Wide Sargasso Sea* in this period, according to Angier, in a quarrel with Leslie.[34] The war years clearly were very hard for Rhys. She did not hear from her daughter for the entire duration of hostilities (1939–45), as Maryvonne had chosen to return to Holland to live with her father in late 1939, while still a teenager. As the war progressed, Rhys received alarming news, that when the Germans invaded Holland Maryvonne had been staying with Jewish friends. It was only in 1945 that Rhys heard her daughter was safe, had worked in the Resistance and been arrested, and now was about to be married. Lenglet had also worked for the Resistance and had been arrested, declared insane and put into an asylum, then prison, then Sachsenhausen concentration camp, and had even survived the notorious death march of 1945.[35]

During the war, Leslie joined the RAF for several years, but he was able to serve at a desk. He died of a heart attack in 1945. Though it is clear that Rhys had the opportunity to work during these years, there were immense stresses: anxiety about her daughter and Lenglet and the loss through death of Leslie's loving support. During and after the war she seems to have worked on short stories and her habitual notebook entries, but after 1939 she entered a long period in which she vanished from public view as a writer and in literary circles was assumed to be dead.

Jean Rhys and Ella Hamer 1946–1966

Angier suggests that Leslie's death, and his active involvement in Rhys's writing life, prevented the publication of a volume of short stories which she had ready in 1945, and that she only published two new stories between 1945 and 1966.[36] In 1947, she married Max Hamer, a cousin of Leslie, who was devoted to her but not a literary man. Their life together was tumultuous, as well as happy. Max was impulsive, looking for ways to make money, which got him into trouble with the law, wrecking his career and ultimately his health.[37] As her alcoholism worsened, Rhys went through some years of fighting with neighbors and tenants living in the house she and Max had in Beckenham, a suburb of south London.[38] Though her family had moved to Britain, she had difficult relationships with many of her relatives. She quarreled or lost touch with several friends, and Maryvonne married a Dutch man and was living in Holland. Whilst Max was in prison, therefore, Rhys spent a good deal of time alone, out of which came a remarkable document, "From a Diary: At the Ropemaker's Arms." She prefaced it with a note, "While for a time I was separated from Max, I lived in rooms above a pub in Maidstone, and there wrote a diary in a little brown copybook. The year was 1947 . . ." (*SP*:129). Angier corrects the date to 1952 (Rhys did not even marry Max until October 1947, and he went to prison in 1950 and served exactly two years of his three-year sentence).[39] "From a Diary" contains "The

Trial of Jean Rhys," in which Rhys is cross-questioned by prosecution and defence lawyers as to her life. She says, "I must write. If I stop writing my life will have been an abject failure to myself. I will not have earned death" (*SP*:133); and, "all of a writer that matters is in the book or books" (*SP*:136). Rhys had a great deal of courage in facing her demons when she could work.

In the late 1950s, she applied herself to completing *Wide Sargasso Sea.* The BBC broadcast a dramatization of part of *Good Morning, Midnight* (May, 1957), and in the process mentioned that she was working on a new novel, which brought Rhys a contract for its publication.[40] In 1949, when an actress, Selma vaz Dias, was seeking permission for the dramatization, there was a strong rumour that Rhys had died. Despite difficult living conditions, (a former tea-room in Cornwall, highly unsuitable during the winter), she persisted with the work, eventually moving to a small bungalow in a village near Exeter, through her brother Edward's generosity in 1960.[41] Her struggle to finish her last novel is vividly recorded in letters, often to her Deutsch editors Francis Wyndham and Diana Athill. Just before it appeared, Max died, after a long period of very poor health and physical dependency.[42]

Jean Rhys 1966–1979

Wide Sargasso Sea was enormously successful. In addition, the story of Rhys's presumed "death" and return to writerly life made for good copy. Though she could easily have stopped writing after this triumph, Rhys worked on her old stories and wrote some new ones, which resulted in two volumes, *Tigers Are Better-Looking* (1968) and *Sleep It Off Lady* (1976), as well as a slim collection of three short pieces, *My Day* (1975), and finally the unfinished autobiography, *Smile Please* (1979). She died in May 1979 after a fall which broke her hip and resulted in an operation.[43]

Rhys was unquestionably a Caribbean writer, but she was also a cosmopolitan, and her work often protests borders and separations. Though she did travel as a young woman, leaving the Caribbean, moving from London to Paris and Europe, most of her adult life was spent imagining places as opposed to going to them.

Rhys lived a very writerly life, full of commitment to the work and obsessive perfectionism about form, and she proved herself bravely capable of extraordinary work in the face of serious difficulties. She was first and foremost a writer, and she "earned her death," as she put it, by doing what she did best to the very end.

Chapter 2

Contexts

Cultural identities

Rhys was culturally complex. She had a Caribbean upbringing and accepted her Celtic ancestry, but she resisted England (English and Anglo-Saxon were synonymous for her). Early direct experience of "this cold, dark country" was so unsettling that she found "my love and longing for books completely left me" (*SP*:90).

Her Welsh father's mother was known as "Irish Granny." A picture of the Catholic Mary Queen of Scots hung over the sideboard in her Anglican parents' house in Roseau. But books popular in middle-class houses in England itself were displayed in her parents' glass-fronted bookcase, like the *Encyclopaedia Britannica* and poetry by English poets both major (Milton and Byron) and mid-level (Crabbe and Cowper) as well as the once-popular but now long-forgotten Felicia Hemans (1793–1835).[1] There were well-known novels that either spread colonial ideas (*Robinson Crusoe*, 1719, *Treasure Island*, 1883) or subtly critiqued them (*Gulliver's Travels*, 1726), or reinforced Christian ideals (*Pilgrim's Progress*, 1678). "Irish Granny" also sent fairy stories and Greek mythology to Rhys herself, who got into trouble with her severe nurse, Meta, for reading *The Arabian Nights*, even though it was an edition suitable for children (*SP*:17, 20–1).

Rhys also had a lifelong love for French literature and culture. Dominica has a strong French-derived cultural identity, as does nearby St Lucia, and neighbor islands Martinique and Guadaloupe are still part of France today. In her story, "The Day They Burned the Books," the young narrator finds that Maupassant's *Fort Comme La Mort* "seemed dull" (*CS*:157) If she had not known French it would simply have been incomprehensible.[2] In 1924, Ford thought Rhys's future was with French literature. He wrote a piece of enjoyable and flirtatious hyberbole for the preface to *The Left Bank*, hoping that "hundreds of years hence," when Rhys's ashes would be recognized as those of a great writer, to whom "the most prominent of the Haute Bourgeoisie of France" would pay homage, "a grain or so of my scattered and forgotten dust may go in too, in the folds."[3] Further, through the relationship with her first husband Jean Lenglet, Rhys extended her connection with Europe, not only through his ties to France and Holland (both his parents were French-speaking Dutch and the Lenglets married in The Hague), but through her experience with him of Vienna and elsewhere in Europe. Their son was born in Paris and their daughter near Brussels. She was educated in Holland after 1927 and made her own life there.

The irony is that, despite her love of Europe and dislike of England, Rhys found success as a writer in England. But to her it was always a chilly and gloomy country which broke her heart twice when she was young (her rejection at Tree's School and Smith's abandonment of her). But then she married two Englishmen, despite years before kneeling down and thanking God for leaving London to marry Lenglet, and making a vow "that I would never go back whatever happened, whatever happened whatsoever" (*SP*:114). It was British reviewers who first recognized her as a gifted new stylist (even if her first books were not economic successes), and eventually she would be highly praised as an "English novelist".[4]

She was also complicated in terms of her sense of race, religious education and class. Partly educated at a Catholic school, she was Anglican in church attendance along with her family. Though white, she felt different from her siblings with her "pale skin and huge staring eyes of no particular colour" (*SP*:14). Eventually, as an adult, she could say, "I can abstract myself from my body" (*SP*:95). In the colonial Caribbean, she belonged to the elite, but in England she was working-class as a chorus girl and an outsider as a Creole. She invented herself several times and longed to break out of the categories to which others consigned her. In her fiction, she explored these tensions and contradictions.

Modernisms

By modernism, used as a literary or generally aesthetic term, we understand a broad and kinetic range of aesthetic innovations and critical responses to literature.[5] In Europe, it has roots in aesthetic experiments as early as the 1880s but its height is generally considered to be just before, during and after the First World War. Often, it is said to represent dislocations caused by intense industrialization, world war, collapsing or changing belief systems and the enormous impact of globalized colonization. It makes its aesthetic strategies visible and rejects the reproduction of surface reality. High Modernist literature provokes the reader to develop new ways of reading.[6] But, whilst it is well known that modernists such as Picasso were inspired by cultures outside Europe (in his case, those of Africa), an idea persists that modernism began as a European movement. However, societies colonized by Europe experienced massive change over a long period, their ancient traditions altered, their people induced or forced to move and make new cultural formations. Transatlantic slavery enforced modernity in the most brutal of ways for those who survived the Middle Passage. Anti-colonial and postcolonial cultures and movements also have contributed greatly to the aesthetic experiments that mark modernism in Europe. There is, then, a plurality of modernisms, inflected by different locales.[7]

Rhys began to write seriously in Paris right at the exciting moment when the Modernist movement was taking the city by storm, and, whilst she walked her own aesthetic road, inevitably she was influenced by ideas vibrant in contemporary literary circles. As Ford noted in his preface to *The Left Bank*, she learned to use a subjective narrative voice and to resist description of locales by reading young French writers in Paris in the early 1920s. She had been in Vienna in 1921, one of the centers of modernism's acceleration in the early 1890s.[8] From the first, she liked to employ familiar modernist strategies such as punctuating a narrative by ellipses and using stream of consciousness to represent the disjointed manner of actual apprehension of experience.[9] She responded to the mechanization of life so associated with urban modernity through her employment of images of machines, as in her story "Outside the Machine."[10] She expressed a subversive response to a world not only hierarchical and indifferent to the individual who refuses to fit into its expectations, but potentially (and often arbitrarily) violent.

Mary Lou Emery rightly points out that Rhys's Caribbean background strongly informs her modernism.[11] Ford intuitively realized that there was something different about Rhys's voice right at the beginning of her literary career, something not from Europe, whose literature, he said, has "a perennial bias toward satisfaction with things as they are" (perhaps because many European writers were from reasonably comfortable backgrounds and had a sense of insider entitlement to their cultural locations). By contrast, he perceptively saw that Rhys's "passion for stating the case of the underdog" was connected to her Antillean origin, a "sympathy" not much present in Western literature.[12] For her, as for other, later Caribbean writers, art needed to be conscious of political dimensions, even with regard to the personal life, and its formal identities were called out by political, cultural and social contexts. Her story "The Day They Burned the Books" is a dramatic representation of the widow of an Englishman ("a decent, respectable, nicely educated coloured woman," *CS*:151), getting rid of the library beloved by her husband by selling some books and burning the rest.[13] Literature is not separated from racial and gender hegemonies in British colonial culture in this story – it is their vehicle. Rhys's development of a modernist aesthetic is deeply informed by her complicated cultural identity.

Literary migrations

Rhys was only on the fringes of Ford's Paris "court" of stellar modernists, though she was helped for a while by his support and tutelage. The short-lived *transatlantic review* was the reason Ford moved to Paris.[14] The writers he published or who supported the journal were truly transatlantic and cosmopolitan: not just Pound, Hemingway, Joyce and Stein, but also e.e. cummings, Joseph Conrad, Paul Valéry, A. E. Coppard and William Carlos Williams. Rhys's first publication, "Vienne" appeared there also.

Rhys's life was roughly chronologically parallel to those of the major modernists Eliot, Ernest Hemingway and Joyce. Joyce was eight years older than Rhys, Eliot two years older, and Hemingway eight years younger. She started publishing her work a little later than they did, and was in her late thirties when her first book was published (1927). Her next three appeared in 1929, 1931 and 1934, a pace commensurate with theirs. Joyce's first book, *Dubliners*, appeared in 1914 when he was thirty-two (though it was written in 1904–7), and *A Portrait of the Artist as a Young Man* was serialized in 1914–15. Eliot's "The Love Song of J. Alfred Prufrock" appeared in 1915, when he was twenty-seven, "Gerontian" in 1920 and his seminal critical essay, "Tradition and the Individual Talent," in 1919.[15] The year 1922 saw both Eliot's *The Waste Land* and Joyce's *Ulysses*. Rhys's first publication, the story "Vienne," appeared in 1924. Hemingway published his first volume of stories, *In Our*

Time, in 1925, when he was twenty-seven. *The Torrents of Spring* and *The Sun Also Rises* appeared the following year, and the stories, *Men Without Women*, in 1927.

Migration was a key element in the lives of a great many major literary modernists whose careers became established in the 1920s. In general, moving from culture to culture facilitates both a disrupted memory of home, which lends itself to modernist collage or interrupted narrative, and the reinvention of self, which contributes to thinking about literary character as potentially contradictory and many-faceted. But though Eliot, Joyce and Hemingway traveled a good deal and lived away from their countries of origin for all or much of their adult lives, their migrations were very different in kind from those of Rhys.[16] Eliot had two cultural and geographic poles in his life: the educated, cultivated U.S.A. and U.K. He was born in St Louis, Missouri, though his paternal family had strong ties to Massachusetts. He had settled in London by 1917. He had a deep interest in Sanskrit and found Hindu and Buddhist thought more satisfying than most European philosophy, but he nevertheless found himself at home in Britain's rather monocultural literary and cultural circles of the early twentieth century.[17] Rhys, by contrast, hated the English and never felt at home in England.

Joyce was born in Dublin, still a British colony in 1882, to a middle-class Catholic family. By 1902, he had abandoned medical school in Dublin to study medicine in Paris, though in 1902–3, during his mother's terminal illness, he returned to Dublin often. Joyce left his homeland early (1904), like Rhys, and he settled in Trieste for ten years. He lived in Zurich from 1915, returning to Trieste in 1919, after the First World War was over. From 1920 to 1940 he lived in Paris. He died in Zurich in 1941. As with Rhys, his work was partly stimulated by being separated from his birthplace, but he wrote about his homeland far more extensively than did Rhys.

Hemingway was born in Illinois and served in the First World War as an ambulance driver. Working as a reporter took him back to Europe. He lived in Paris on and off during the first half of the 1920s (after which he lived in Spain and Key West, visited Africa for safaris, and finally returned to his roots in the U.S. mid-West). He depicted the trials of being male in three continents: bold travel to find new experience is a key theme in his work. But his fictional self-exiles are more expatriate than migrant.

Rhys represented Anglophone expatriates and migrants (for example from the Antilles and Morocco). But she problematized the expatriates (mainly because of their implicitly colonizing, exploitative tendencies), and made clear that her migrants were marginalized within their new culture. Her protagonists are isolated and numbed by their emotional traumas so that they often can scarcely register the immediate world around them, let alone go any further afield.

Thinking about these parallels and differences is very helpful in identifying Rhys's particular modernist complexity. She was skeptical about the ability of the outsider to ever belong in another culture, and more particularly a Creole woman trying to cope with the sexism, racism and class divisions of early twentieth-century Britain. But Rhys did reference Joyce and Eliot in her work, showing that she was aware of their particular and individual modernisms.[18]

Pioneer women artists outside polite society: Rhys, Colette and Edith Piaf

The lives and work of two French women, a writer and a singer, one born seventeen years before Rhys and the other a quarter of a century after, can add an important dimension to reading Rhys. Colette (1873–1954) is uncannily comparable to Rhys in a number of ways. Her mother's maternal ancestry was Martiniquan. Colette said that her Caribbean ancestors were "cocoa-harvesters from the colonies", and her grandfather was a "ginger-colored gorilla."[19] She performed in music-hall. She had one daughter, but most of her time and attention went to her work. She wrote about a gigolo in *Chéri* (1919) and *The Last of Chéri*; Rhys's René in *Good Morning, Midnight* is a gigolo. Her work, like Rhys's, was criticized in some quarters for portraying seedy, disreputable characters. They both developed important personal relationships that facilitated their work. Colette's husband Willy stole her work but got her to write prolifically. She later lived with Missy (Sophìe-Mathilde-Adéle-Denise de Morny, Marquìse de Belboeuf), a lesbian transvestite who was very supportive, and finally married a younger man who loved her writing. Like Rhys, she lived through tumultuous times (two world wars and the Depression) without much witnessing them in her fiction. Most importantly, her memoir *Mes apprentissages* (1936) contains details very close to Rhys's story of the beginning of her writing life in *Smile Please* (so close it seems likely that Rhys read Colette's text, and she certainly kept a passage from it in her papers).[20] Colette speaks of writing in exercise books and then putting them away for two years in the bottom of a drawer. Rhys's similar account describes putting exercise books in the bottom of a suitcase and not looking at them for seven years. Colette, like Rhys, wrote many pieces of short fiction and their structure, style and sometimes subject matter reverberate with many of Rhys's stories set in Paris.[21]

But for the most part their work has a very different feel. Colette's descriptions of people and places have a much richer sensuousness (new readers of Rhys are often dismayed by the lack of sexual and other sensuous pleasures in her characters). Colette's sense of the body, or of a plant in a garden, or food or drink, is far more earthy, perhaps most evidently in *Le pur et l'impur.*[22] Rhys was profoundly shaped by the middle-class sexual strictures of the colonial and heavily Catholic Dominica into which she was born. Rhys points out in *Smile Please* that, whereas little white children of both sexes were allowed quite a lot of freedom from clothes, and boys and girls interacted, later white girls were heavily covered up both for school and church, despite the heat. On top of which, molested as a teenager by her mother's friend Mr. Howard, she felt she had to keep quiet about it.

Edith Piaf (1915–63) was a quarter of a century younger than Rhys. She died in her late forties, during Rhys's silent period. She had outstanding singing talent, but a tragic life. Her parents were performers (her mother a street singer, her father in the circus), but her family gave her no emotional stability (her mother abandoned her, her father was intermittently capable of caring for her, one grandmother was a cook in a brothel and the other trained fleas for the circus, neither being appropriate surrogate mothers). Like Rhys she endured the loss of a young child to whom she had not been able to give sustained maternal care (her daughter died at three years old), and had a turbulent emotional life (losing the man she most cared about, Marcel Cerdan, in an air crash). She also had problems with alcoholism and other drug abuse. But what Piaf and Rhys shared above all else was a refusal to give up their work, despite enormous difficulties, considerably caused by their own personal problems.

None of these women started out planning an artistic career. They all have strong ties to music-hall, the marginal and transgressive space which gave actresses just slightly more social standing than prostitutes but which also offered an uncharted freedom of sexual expression and adventure, even if at a cost. That experience was an important foundation for their unconventional artistic achievements.

The woman writer

Ford said unequivocally of Rhys's early work that she had a "singular instinct for form . . . possessed by singularly few writers of English and by almost no English women writers" (by this he probably meant those immediately contemporary with Rhys, but it is an indefensible statement).[23] But the issue in identifying a writer as a woman is how indeed that plays out in terms of aesthetics, not just subject matter. H.D. (Hilda Doolittle), the Imagist poet (born 1882), and Djuna Barnes (born 1892) were both contemporaries of Rhys: both were more sexually and aesthetically unconventional. H.D. was more sustainedly part of contemporary literary culture than was Rhys. Barnes's fiction, like Rhys's, depicts outsiders and bohemians in the city (Paris and New York). Virginia Woolf, born 1882, the same year as James Joyce, had published five novels, including *Mrs Dalloway* (1922) and *To the Lighthouse* (1927), by the time Rhys's first book came out. It is productive to read Virginia Woolf's use of stream of consciousness alongside that of Rhys, but their worlds are very different. Woolf's famous comment that a woman needs a room of her own in which to work implies that a woman can afford such a thing or have it provided by someone else. In both Rhys's life and her fiction, the temporary, cheap rented room provides no encouragement to pursue the higher things of life.

Rhys adopted a first name as her writing name which, depending on the context, could signify either gender (Jean as French is a man's name, and as English a woman's). Rhys was never a feminist and indeed often had more difficult relations with women than with men. She was ambivalent about the "woman writer," whom she considered particularly hated in literary circles. Her difficulties with women writers are evident in her letters (*L*:29, 32–33). Her male characters (most especially the unnamed husband in *Wide Sargasso Sea*) often comment on her female protagonists in ways that help balance her fiction and protect it against gender bias. Rhys herself appreciated men. She was anxious in a letter to her friend Peggy Kirkaldy that she might have given the impression that her husband Max was "a bit of a pansy," when, "Au contraire. He is a very male creature . . ." (*L*:75); but she also thought that he was "heart-rendingly naive," an example of which was that "he hates my writing" (*L*:75), which had to have been an issue. As in her complex assessment of Max, Rhys does not flatten her fictional characters into a good versus bad script, and though her sense of gender inequalities is acute in her writing, she portrays the victim as often complicit in her exploitation. The longest narrative in her most famous novel, *Wide Sargasso Sea*, is a man's.

Yet feminist criticism contributed a great deal to Rhys's recognition as an important writer. For such critics, Rhys's work represents the power of gender norms in culture (in Paris and Britain in the first half of the twentieth century, and then in the colonial Caribbean). Nancy Harrison, in *Jean Rhys and the Novel as Women's Text*, a feminist approach to Rhys's work, suggests that reviewers and critics claiming objectivity (often men) subject women writers to "an especially rigorous examination of their credentials."[24]

Feminist readings of Rhys have tried to read her work through a different lens. Caroline Rody insightfully reads the relation between *Wide Sargasso Sea* and Charlotte Brontë's *Jane Eyre* (1847) as both a kind of daughterly affiliation (woman writer recognizing a literary ancestor) and an attack on the canonical Brontë text, which was created from within the heart of British imperial culture.[25] More dubious is the claim that Rhys somehow had an unconscious feminism (despite the fact that, as a political position, feminism is a call to conscious action).[26] But to read Rhys as *simply* creating marginalized or oppressed women characters also erases complexities that mark Rhys's women characters as modern, contradictory people who often aid and abet their own exploitation.

Sidonie Smith (1987) theorizes autobiography as an "androcentric genre . . . the public story of the public life" (this was of course written before the recent vogue for memoirs about the most private aspects of private lives, written as much by men as by women). Smith profiles a woman's autobiography as following an established male pattern familiar to readers : "a pattern of progressive stages . . . how she has become who she is: the childhood that moved her toward some vocation, her educational and intellectual experiences, her entrance into the public arena . . .", replicating the "prevailing ideology of male selfhood."[27] Rhys's *Smile Please* certainly sets out to portray her journey from childhood to writerly adulthood, reflecting this model, though the book was never completed.

It is wise to remember that Rhys was both conventional about gender (her lifelong love of makeup and pretty clothes), and unconventional (her scorn of typically feminine domesticity). Rather than making Rhys a "woman writer" in any simple sense, realizing how complexly she represents the performance of gender in her texts enables us to realize far more of their richness and subtlety.

The colonial postcolonial

Rhys was born into a British colonial society and traveled as an impressionable teenager to the heart of the Empire at a time when it was still in its ascendancy. She experienced a Paris in which the center of cultural life was French, but in which individuals from cultures marginalized by French imperialism tried to find a place. She lived long enough to witness the ending of the British Empire and the flow of immigrants from former colonies into Britain during the fifties and sixties. Though what we think of as the postcolonial, in culture and intellectual life, did not begin to come into prominence until the mid-twentieth century, in cultures battling imperialism there were early signs of literary resistance to it. Declan Kiberd, discussing Irish literature, makes a distinction between European and postcolonial artists: "... post-colonial artists, born as copies, were determined to die as originals ... (t)he modernizers from Europe sought to expose the myths of traditional societies to the scrutiny of analytic reason, but they never dismantled the myths which bound them to their own culture." He goes on to say of Joyce's masterpiece *Ulysses* that it is "often treated as a definitive account of the mind of modern Europe in 1922," but that means understanding that Europe was nothing "without its colonial holdings."[28]

Rhys's career can be seen as framed by the emergence of two writers, one a product of imperialism and its promulgator through fiction, and the other making a direct engagement with such colonial distortion. Joyce Cary's *Mister Johnson* appeared in 1939, the same year as *Good Morning, Midnight*, a time when British imperial power was still at its height. His career as a British colonial administrator in Nigeria was over before he started to write. Distinguished Nigerian novelist Chinua Achebe is honoured as a founding father of modern African literature. His writing career began in angry response to *Mister Johnson*'s colonialist vision of Nigeria (*Things Fall Apart*, 1958).[29] Rhys's long silence during the 1940s and 1950s occurred during this shift from colonial to postcolonial writing.

In the mid-twentieth century Anglophone Caribbean literature became a significant new canon. Major texts appearing in the 1950s included Samuel Selvon's novel *A Brighter Sun* (1952), George Lamming's novel *In the Castle of My Skin* (1953) and V. S. Naipaul's collection of stories, *Miguel Street* (1959).[30] All three of these writers had migrated to Britain hoping to find publishers and markets for their work. But Rhys remained silent throughout the 1950s. So by the time *Wide Sargasso Sea* appeared (1966), critics and scholars had begun to recognize Caribbean literature as an emerging literature of great excellence. But just as the reader needs to be careful in reading Rhys through the lens of gender, so it is necessary to be attentive to the complexities of Rhys as either Caribbean or postcolonial writer.

During the completion of *Wide Sargasso Sea*, to help her get inside the character of Antoinette's English husband, "Rochester," Rhys wrote a poem, "Obeah Nights," in his voice (*L*:264–6). Obeah, the belief system in the Caribbean, was created during and after slavery, and is usually understood to be the result of syncretism of multiple West African systems of consultation with spiritual practitioners (and is therefore a one on one consultation, not a religious community like a congregation). It was regarded by the British as evil and primitive, and they suppressed obeah practitioners, though Hesketh

Bell, Administrator of Dominica, interestingly wrote that he felt the "witch-pots" of Devon and Dorset in England were another influence on obeah, as well as old Irish "superstitions".[31] Rhys lived in a village in Devon during the time she worked on *Wide Sargasso Sea*, and felt that villagers there believed in witchcraft. But Rhys neither affirmed nor denied obeah in the novel: she both represents "Rochester" 's colliding skepticism about and fear of obeah and Antoinette's willingness to use obeah, even despite Christophine's warnings. Thus obeah enables the reader to see the complexity of both "Rochester" 's self-betrayals and Antoinette's self-wounding battle to hold his affection.

Rhys's complex identity and experience informed her sense of the world so strongly that she resisted writing only one side of any story. She is both colonial and postcolonial, white but Creole, and she expressed views and made remarks that demonstrate these contradictions.[32] She was often wry about the woman writer. Rhy's major characters often have a contradictory and hardly stable sense of self. She often used irony, a key tool of the postcolonial writer, which permits the apparently accommodating public address to power to be undermined by the subversive underlying meaning. Her achievement is the more impressive when we think of the ways that much modernist fiction held onto the old idea of the individual as a coherent entity, despite recognizing a new social instability within which that individual must function. Postmodernism recognizes the fluidity and contingency of individual identity. Rhys, coping with all the different strands of her identity and cultural affiliations, would have instantly understood postmodernism's gloss on the idea of the self, and this makes her very much of our immediate moment. Robert Antoni's markedly postmodern novel, *Blessed is the fruit*, was partly inspired by Rhys's *Wide Sargasso Sea.*[33]

Published and unpublished: Rhys's notebooks and manuscripts

There is a large body of Rhys's manuscripts, notebooks and letters, as well as related materials such as reviews of her work, in the Rhys Collection at the McFarlin Library, University of Tulsa, Oklahoma. Given the number of times Rhys moved in her life, not only from country to country but from house to house, often with little money, it is clear that much of this precious material survived because of the careful custodianship of publishers and literary friends, who, for example, saved drafts of stories typed by assistants (in Rhys's later years), as well as letters. The survival of the notebooks is, however, more remarkable and attests to their value for Rhys as source material. There are several major ways in which the unpublished material can help with understanding Rhys's work. Firstly, multiple drafts of stories demonstrate her working method. Secondly, the notebooks demonstrate her lifelong commitment to turning painful experience into raw material to be mined for her work. Thirdly, her unpublished novel "Triple Sec" is very rewarding to read alongside *Voyage in the Dark* as well as other texts.

An example of the first category are the variant drafts of "The Imperial Road," an account of Rhys's visit to Dominica with her second husband Leslie Tilden Smith, in 1936. There are seven in the Rhys Collection at the University of Tulsa (one handwritten and the others typed). Some have titles, "Mother Mount Calvary" and "Return of the Native" (a nice recall of Thomas Hardy's novel).[34] The process of final revision was extremely detailed and meticulous for Rhys, as these versions clearly demonstrate: she inserted punctuation last. In a letter, Rhys said of stories she was working on in the mid-1940s, "I tried too hard for one thing, and was so afraid of offending that I wrote and rewrote the life out of the things" (*L*:44). In another letter, she confessed, "I can write mediocre poetry so easily, and labour so over prose" (*L*:271). Unpublished works help us understand the published work in important ways. There are details in "The Imperial Road" that appear in *Wide Sargasso Sea*: two examples are a woman who wears a dress with a trailing hem and a bright turban (similar to Christophine's dress in the novel), and key details in the portrayal of the girl which return in the character of Amélie. The unpublished manuscript "Triple Sec" clearly provided raw material for Rhys's later fiction, most especially *Voyage in the Dark*.

The notebooks are also extremely important. Their lack of punctuation shows Rhys always began with free-flowing thoughts interrupting themselves: "After two or three doses of this drug because that's what it was I no longer struggled" (The Black Exercise Book, story of Mr. Howard); "in bitterness and loneliness so complete" (the opening of the Black Exercise Book). A sentence which appears in *Smile Please*, "It was divided into two parts, one for the white people in front, the other for the black people at the back: there was a space between," largely originates in an exercise book (Red) as "It was divided into two parts one for the white people the other for the black people at the back."

From examining her process, we can learn how hard Rhys worked to become the outstanding stylist she was, giving her work vigilant attention to detail and, the closer the text came to completion, pursuing a relentless perfectionism.

Making the "truth"

In a 1968 interview, at the height of media attention on her, Rhys explained that "glimpses of happiness and wealth" diverted her from the desire to write, because when "one is happy one is absorbed in it," and if you try to write the truth, "then it remains the truth for all time," which is the way to avoid the work becoming dated.[35] She mined her complex self for many characters, none of which was entirely Jean Rhys, but all of which express a convincing experiential "truth," or honesty. She is a writer who teaches us how to use the personal life for fiction without getting sunk into the mire of subjectivity, and how to avoid the merely ephemeral and local without losing a sense of the location of the stories she tells.

Chapter 3

Texts

The Left Bank (1927)

Rhys's first book was a collection of short fiction, a common apprenticeship among novelists. In these early stories, she established major characteristics of her style. She continued to write short fiction all her life.

The collection consists of twenty-two stories, some very brief. Though the title indicates the bohemian, intellectual, artistic Paris that Rhys experienced most with Ford, there are pieces set in or which refer to the Caribbean ("Mixing Cocktails," "Again the Antilles" and "Trio"). In "La Grosse Fifi," the central character's name is Roseau, the capital of Dominica. "Trio," in its Antillean exile theme, is the bridge to two Dominican memoir pieces, "Mixing Cocktails" and "Again the Antilles." But if the Caribbean is an important point of reference in this collection, Paris is central. To be there in the early 1920s as an artist was to be at the birth of High Modernism, and even though Rhys was never a joiner of groups or movements, literary or not, her association with Ford temporarily put her right in the center of parties and literary discussions in cafés and restaurants such as the famous Café du Dôme (more simply Le Dôme), mentioned at the opening of "The Blue Bird." Rhys identified Montparnasse as "Chelsea, London, with a large dash of Greenwich

Village, New York, to liven it, and a slight sprinkling of Moscow, Christiania and even of Paris to give incongruous local colourings" (*CS*:16–17). Rhys had not visited the US at that time, but Greenwich Village was often compared to Montparnasse by cosmopolitan people who knew both.

The cryptic, wry tone that is a hallmark of much of Rhys's writing is already established in her early stories. Diana Athill remarks that "there is more humour in Jean Rhys's observation of life than is usually recognized" (*CS*:ix). The stories in *TLB* frequently express a subversive attitude to those who dominate or feel themselves superior to others. In "Tout Montparnasse and a Lady," the central character is an American fashion artist "who was there to be thrilled" (*CS*:17). She has read Francis Carco's portraits of Paris street life, one of which Rhys translated.[1] Disliking Anglo-Saxons, this woman nevertheless looks for excitement where Anglo-Saxons go. She stares at a man, thinking he is on drugs, when he is actually imagining his next creative work. Annoyed, thinking she is a journalist, he says: "Oh God! How I hate women who write! How I *hate* them!" (*CS*:17). Rhys has some fun describing the "slightly strained expressions characteristic of the Anglo-Saxon." They try to unwind and enjoy the music, but like "people engaged in some difficult but extremely important gymnastic exercise" (*CS*:16). The men are young, the women not so young, "with that tendency to be thick about the ankles and incongruous about the shoes, which is nearly always to be found in the really intelligent woman" (*CS*:16).

In "A Spiritualist," an emotionally obtuse and exploitative Commandant's persistent self-delusions are neatly and comically skewered. A chunk of marble mysteriously crashes into the apartment of his dead mistress whilst he is there: he thinks she is reminding him that he promised to get a white marble tombstone for her, but a woman he knows comments, "How furious that poor Madeleine must have been that she missed you!" (*CS*:9).

The ironic "In a Café" portrays both French customers and foreign tourists listening to "middle-aged, staid" musicians who match the decor of the café. A stout man in evening dress begins to sing, looking "self-confident, eager and extraordinarily vulgar." His song is about *les grues*, the tarts who are so easily sentimentalized for their hard lives and fragile, available femininity. In the song, three stages are observed, the way the girl becomes a *grue*, her emotional generosity, and the absolute indifference from one of her former lovers when she is wretched and in great need. His sentimental tribute is met with much applause but then a withdrawal into awkwardness: women attend to their makeup, men drink and "looked sideways" (*CS*:14). The singer sells a couple of copies of his song, and then the mood changes. The next song is to be American, "Mommer loves Popper . . . ." (*CS*:15), on a much safer if more infantile emotional level. The brief story "Hunger" is much more acerbic: it reminds Rhys's well-fed readers that they are entertained by horror: "I have never gone without food for more than five days, so I cannot amuse you any longer" (*CS*:44).

The early stories rehearse a major later Rhys theme: marginalization of poor young women exploited by an indifferent elite. "Mannequin" is about the doll-like models, human "flowers," who work for an expensive couture house in Paris, a place where tiring work and economic exploitation are hidden under the façade of pretty girls showing off in pretty clothes. Those who come to buy are often foreign (Dutch, South American, American, English), attracted by the legend of French style.

Rhys often reveals that the inner reality of a character is far more interesting than surface impressions. Her initial descriptions are usually very spare, sometimes to take the reader in. In "Illusion," Miss Bruce, a painter, is depicted through few physical details, "tall, thin," "large bones and hands and feet," a face bare of powder and therefore shining, "beautifully washed . . . with here and there a few rather lovable freckles" (*CS*:2). She is literally a "shining example of what . . . British character and training can do" and resists the Parisian "cult of beauty" (*CS*:1). But when she is ill, the narrator is sent to collect some personal things for her, and finds in her wardrobe a marvelous collection of highly feminine, brightly colored dresses, her secret passion. By the story's end, Miss Bruce is well again, and appraising the hands and arms of a girl "in her gentlemanly manner" (*CS*:5).

This subversion of gender stereotypes is repeated in "The Blue Bird": Carlo, an English expatriate in Paris, is a woman with a voice "as deep as a man's," the narrow shoulders and hips "of a fragile schoolgirl," "faithful" eyes, and a "bitter and tormented mouth" (*CS*:61). She has had a tragic love affair with a "Bad Man" and now sees a man she calls "my Arab" who has a beauty spot on his cheek (*CS*:65).

Rhys experiments with both first- and third-person narration. She would go on in her novels to use both. Some of her short pieces are more personal essay than short story. "Learning to be a Mother" is a very spare account of the birth of her first child, William Owen.[2] The narrative voice in "Hunger" speaks directly to the reader with a laconic tone which is horrifying: "On the third day one feels sick; on the fourth, one starts crying very easily . . . A bad habit that; it sticks" (*CS*:43). In "A Night" a woman speaks of her temptation to commit suicide. Both Antilles stories are first person. The tone of memoir is reinforced by the resemblance of the house in "Mixing Cocktails" to Bona Vista, the house Rhys's father bought in the hills north of Roseau in Dominica. "Again the Antilles" very effectively portrays verbal skirmishes in the lively Dominican press at the end of the nineteenth century, by which the powerful "mulatto" elite and the white English colonials challenged each other. "Vienne," by far the longest story here, follows the first heady and then turbulent period in Rhys's first marriage to Jean Lenglet, when he took a job of secretary-interpreter to the Interallied Commission in Vienna shortly after the First World War ended and then got into trouble over art and currency dealings. It has a strong first-person narrative and is told in a terse voice, often sounding like a journal, with margin interruptions as if this were a piece of modernist poetry:

> The girls were well dressed, not the slightest bit made up–
> that seemed odd after Paris.
> Gorgeous blue sky and green trees and a good orchestra.
> And heat and heat.
> I was cracky with joy of life that summer of 1921.
> I'd darling muslin frocks covered with frills and floppy hats–
> or a little peasant dress and no hat. (*CS*:101)

The narrator goes through a good deal in hoping for financial security and then gradually faces the fact that her husband is on the wrong side of the law, just as Lenglet was: ". . . as I touched him my courage, my calm, my insensibility left me and I felt a sort of vague and bewildered fright" (*CS*:115).

Ford complained that Rhys had little sense of place in the preface he wrote for *The Left Bank*: "I tried . . . very hard to induce the author . . . to introduce some sort of topography of that region, bit by bit, into her sketches . . . but would she do it? No!"[3] He noticed a sense of locale in her Caribbean landscapes but he could not find one in her stories set in Montparnasse, London or Vienna. Rhys does, however, clearly map the locations of her stories, and in later Rhys texts these would again be important. In *The Left Bank*, there are four geographical clusters: the Latin Quarter, Montparnasse, the Left Bank and a prison somewhere within a tram ride of the city; Rhys's birthplace of Dominica; the South of France; and Vienna, Budapest and Prague. Miss Bruce lives in "The Quarter." The "little flat" of the young mistress of the Commandant in "A Spiritualist" is on the Place de L'Odéon, which is just north of the Luxembourg Gardens. "In a Café" is again vaguely located in "the Quarter," but in "Tout Montparnasse and a Lady" the *bal musette* is on the Rue St. Jacques, which runs right past the Sorbonne. "Mannequin" is set in a high-class dress salon on the affluent north bank of the Seine, in the Place Vendôme, a location where bohemian girls from the Quarter might find work serving wealthy patrons. "In the Luxemburg Gardens" (*sic*) is as much about the ambience of the gardens as the brief sketch of a young man there. In "Tea with an Artist," the painter

Verhausen lives in "the real Latin Quarter which lies north of the Montparnasse district and is shabbier and not cosmopolitan yet" (*CS*:30). "Trio" is set in a restaurant in Montparnasse. "In the Rue de L'Arrivée" again references an actual street, running south from the Boulevard Montparnasse. "The Blue Bird" takes place in the famous Café du Dôme restaurant, 108, Boulevard du Montparnasse. The place in a Rhys story is very often represented as a way of demonstrating emotion in a narrator or main character. This determines what will be noticed (perhaps certain colors or details of dress or behavior, or a pervasive depressive erasure of such details). But Rhys's close attention to geography helps identify many small details that subtly illuminate her characters.

These stories are an early demonstration of her mastery of precise and effective use of language, always very economical: "Fifi was not terrific except metaphorically" (*CS*:80); "(f)rom the small, blurred glass her eyes stared back at her, darkly circled, the whites slightly bloodshot, the clear look of youth going-gone" ("In the Rue de L'Arrivée, *CS*:51). The style of the stories is strongly modernist, leaving many gaps for the reader to fill in, often more collage than linear development. In her expression of power and powerlessness, and the role of language in sustaining inequities, Rhys anticipates postcolonial perspectives, as in "Again the Antilles," when a colonial Englishman's patronizing letter appears in the newspaper complaining about the "ignorant of another race and colour." The narrator adds, "Mr Mugrave had really written 'damn niggers'" (*CS*:41).

Rhys also makes the reader experience Paris through her references to or use of French. In "A Night," the female narrator is haunted by a phrase, written in Rhys's text as if on a billboard, "Le Saut dans l'Inconnu," which she remembers reading as red letters on a black ground. It means "a leap in the dark," but is never translated in the story. In "In the Rue de l'Arrivée" a man approaches the protagonist. Although she gives the first part of the dialogue in English, Rhys makes clear that the two characters actually speak in French by the latter part of the brief exchange: " '*Allez-vous en*' she said fiercely . . . She heard him say softly, as if meditatively, '*Pauvre petite, va*' " (*CS*:53).

This collection has been seen as apprentice work, but there are several very strong stories, such as "La Grosse Fifi." A troubled young woman, Roseau, meets Fifi, an ageing and preposterously costumed woman who is in love with a much younger gigolo. Fifi loves French poetry, and is extremely romantic. After the gigolo fatally stabs her, he claims she attacked him first with a knife because he told her of his impending marriage. The story ends with Roseau's realization of the irony of a piece of French poetry Fifi had given her in which a speaker's life is put in the hands of a lover. The story weaves together several themes (disappointed love, female ageing and isolation, the role of literature in emotional life). It demonstrates Rhys's early remarkable style: "as she swam into the room like a big vessel with all sails set, three, four, five would follow in her wake" (*CS*:89).

Quartet (1929)

Angier claims that Ford Madox Ford and Jean Rhys "were perhaps the two greatest artists of self-pity in English fiction, never more so than in *When the Wicked Man* and *Quartet*."[4] But, precisely in order to make this first novel distanced enough from the painful emotional raw material from which it was fashioned, Rhys imposed a tight structure, identified by the title *Quartet*, with its clever reflection of the four major characters. Despite the centrality of Marya, the title suggests carefully orchestrated interactions with something of the deliberately patterned and emotionally choreographed nature of chamber music.The book had another title for its English debut (*Postures* 1928), but Angier notes that *Quartet* was Rhys's first choice,[5] and it clearly enabled her to keep a firm grasp on the story.

There are twenty-three numbered chapters, most subdivided by both asterisks and gaps in the text. The resulting ellipses enable Rhys to minimize the clutter of logistical detail. Most chapters have a few main divisions (between two and four), but there is often further ellipsis within a section. An asterisk indicates a more major shift in time and circumstances. Chapter 5 portrays one continuous evening from one point of view and so needs no sectioning. Chapter 7 begins with Marya visiting Stephan in the prison in Fresnes, a tram ride outside Paris. She sees how prison is changing him and tells him the Heidlers have invited her to stay with them, which Stephan insists she should do despite her objections. This is a really key moment of dramatic irony. A break in the text sets Marya walking back to the tram for Paris in a separate space, which is appropriate because she has dismissed her concerns over the Heidlers. Another break conveys a time lapse, and the receipt of a letter from her aunt in England with five pounds and a request not to be bothered again. Thus this chapter's sections move Marya along from refusal to go to the Heidlers to a realization that she has no other reasonable option, since she has no money. Chapter 10 has four major sections, three of them marked by asterisks. The first of these sections is divided into three by ellipses, to signify the shifts from the group of three (Marya, Heidler and Lois), to two (Marya and Heidler), and finally one (Marya alone in her bedroom, spooked by her apprehension of Heidler's sexual intentions to think of ways to defeat them such as bolting the door or getting away). Then an asterisk marks time passing (to the next day). Marya avoids Lois and plans to meet her friend Cairn. In this short section, she realizes she longs "for joy" (*Q*:74). Stephan is in prison and she is alone. It seems she will weaken with regard to Heidler. Another asterisk and space (ellipsis) takes us to the meeting with Cairn, who is clear-sighted about Heidler, though Marya still wants to believe he is kind. After another asterisk, Marya is back at the Heidlers' apartment where Heidler tries to seduce her. The last section of the chapter has no subvisions, because it tracks one continuous scene during which Marya tries to distract Heidler (by asking for a cigarette), and finally stops him by telling him Lois has come home. So the asterisks mark particularly key emotional developments and disruptions in Marya's path towards the affair with Heidler.

Though the narrative voice is third person and Marya is central to the whole text, there are many shifts of perspective. At first we observe Marya from the outside, as if she is in the opening shot of a film, but soon we see the world from her point of view.[6] There are one or two moments when she is not present (the reader is with the Heidlers as they wait for her to arrive, with Cairn as he writes a note to Marya in a bar, and with Mr. Rolls and his guests at the Bal du Printemps), but these few absences only make Marya the more central to the story. We hear Heidler, Lois and Stephan speak to Marya, so we know what they choose to express about their feelings, but we have a much larger emotional vocabulary for Marya because we are told what she cannot or will not express or does not understand but intensely feels: "she looked at them with calmness, clear-sightedly, freed for one moment from her obsessions of love and hatred" (*Q*:97); "She had meant to tell him 'I love you. You aren't making any mistake about that, are you?' But all she said was 'Please will you draw the curtains?'" (*Q*:112); "When they were seated in the Restaurant de Versailles she was still thinking uneasily about the hat, because it seemed symbolical of a new attitude" (*Q*:113). Confronted with first-person narrative, many ordinary readers want to feel some attraction to the voice that interprets the story. But Marya is more remote than passionate, emotionally and morally confused and often careless. The reader needs to appreciate the novel's style rather than looking to like the main character.

Rhys's style draws subtle attention to itself, in the way poetry does. She employs poetic techniques, such as heightened rhythms, like alliteration and assonance or repetition, as well as figurative language. Marya suffers in the Hôtel du Bosphore, and describes her feelings for Heidler in these terms: "(t)hen her obsession gripped her, arid, torturing, gigantic, possessing her as utterly as the longing for water possesses someone who is dying of thirst" (*Q*:117). These exact words return later on, when she returns to the same room, and relives her relationship with Heidler in a horrific way (Q:145). Before the earlier passage, she can keep her mind a blank for ten seconds, and by the time it reappears, she can manage that for thirty seconds, showing that she is slightly improved. The language suggests much through its sound patterns, such as the employment of assonance, as in "(t)he unutterably sweet peace of giving in" (*Q*:107), or alliteration, "When she had posted the pneumatique" (*Q*:146), "looked doubtfully into the dark dining room of the hotel" (*Q*:158). These cadences heighten the language and emphasize reverberative details.

The text foregrounds multilingual, that is, transnational life, so the reader must think about which language is being spoken at a given time. Stephan is Polish, speaks English, and adopts an American accent when nervous, which is an interesting sign that he has had reason to conceal his national identity. Marya and Stephan mainly use French with each other. But the emotional trauma of visiting him in prison makes Marya unable to speak it. The text emphasizes languages and accents (French, English, American). Cairn, an American short-story writer, uses French tags in his conversation with Marya. Rhys includes waiters and others who speak French, made perfectly understandable in the context of the narrative without the necessity of translation. They particularly would have alerted the reader in the late 1920s to the fact that this is not entirely familiar space and that the British reader's own likely monolingual expectations were not going to be indulged by Rhys.

Rhys uses juxtapositions to emphasize character traits that drive the plot: Marya is referred to as a child, and Stephan admits to crying like a boy; Stephan seems freer in a sense in prison, and Marya in prison at the Heidlers. Images are also often amusingly subversive, the way women (and others) without power have to think about those who control them if they are not to be violently angry. Marya thinks Heidler's nose lengthens as he speaks. This is an unspoken reference to Pinocchio and lying – he has just said that Lois is very fond of Marya (*Q*:114). He looks to her "exactly like a picture of Queen Victoria," a damning connection to not only imperial power, and homely female looks, but extremely controlled emotions.

Art is also an important connective theme in the novel. It can be practical, like the photographs that Bernadet enlarges for a living, gorgeous, like the amethyst necklace Stephan and another man discuss, or sinister, like Napoleon's sabre, laid down "naked" by Stephan on Marya's bed, a vaguely menacing metaphor (like the sword that lies between two lovers to keep them chaste; *Q*:20). There is a chain of references to sensation, which are often disturbing (torture, numbness), and repeated references to light, darkness or greyness and to warmth or cold. Lois has a "dark face" (*Q*:97, 99); Heidler's face looks "white and lined" (*Q*:100); and when distressed Marya's face is "greyish" (*Q*:124). Dreams and ghosts are another important chain of images: leaving Stephan in prison, Marya says she feels like a "grey ghost" (*Q*:57).

Creatures are particularly important and denote emotional realities and intensities with great economy. Marya, horribly affected by drink and drugs, imagines herself as small as a fly (flies are usually reviled and rejected, anything but beautiful, but here the fly is frail and wanting to live). Lois moves her head like a "bird picking up crumbs" (*Q*:59). References to animals are frequent and key. Marya is "a strange animal or . . . a strayed animal" (*Q*:11). Her desire for joy is "like some splendid caged animal" (*Q*:74). As she sees her bedroom door open, and Heidler makes his move, she has the "(f)right of an animal caught in a trap" (*Q*:90). She claims she would "fight like a wild animal" if anyone locked her up, but Stephan says everyone becomes a wild animal after they are let out, himself included (*Q*:136). This relates to the caged fox (*Q*:160). Stephan is as "(n)atural as an animal" (*Q*:60) early on and has something "wolf-like" about him at the end of the novel. In prison he is like "some bright-eyed animal" (*Q*:56). Lois has the eyes of a "well-trained domestic animal" (*Q*:107), and makes Marya think of someone who would imagine a mouse enjoys being played with by a cat (*Q*:62). The warder at the prison "snarled" (*Q*:109). When Heidler says no-one knows about his affair with Marya, she says his "crest ought to be an ostrich" (*Q*:120). Heidler is "a swine" (Q:124). Marya lies in Heidler's arms "quivering and abject . . . like some unfortunate dog abasing itself before its master" (*Q*:131). If people are animals, animals can be treated as if they are people, like the "minute and hairy dog" which is "kissed . . . passionately" (*Q*:139) by its owner.

In a directly ironical use of the literary convention of pastoral, Marya wakes in the mornings in the sordid Hôtel du Bosphore to the sound of a "man with a flock of goats who passed under her window every morning about half-past ten, playing a frail little tune on a pipe" (*Q*:111).[7] His music fascinates her, because it is "thin, high, sweet," "like water running in the sun," not intended to entertain or to pursue artistic ambitions, but merely to keep the sheep in order (so he is like an ancient shepherd giving the world unintentional poetry, in a twist on the pastoral tradition). Marya thinks his music "persistent as the hope of happiness." This is still listened for against all reason, just as she still listens as the music fades.

Rhys uses tiny touches of color and design to indicate emotions. Marya remembers a yellow dress Stephan once bought her, in Belgium, which made her feel "like a flower" (*Q*:164). But she is disturbed by the "vaguely erotic" wallpaper in her room in the Hôtel de Bosphore, which has mauve, green and yellow flowers on a black background (*Q*:111). Pink and purple are worn by women trying to appeal to men: the bedcover in this room is pink, and even Lois Heidler wears it. In the country house at Brunoy, the wallpaper in Marya's room has "ridiculous rabbits" chasing each other on it, like a child's room (*Q*:99). Makeup is either done well, "(c)rimson was where crimson should be" (*Q*:8), or badly, "the powder and rouge stood out in clownish patches" (*Q*:124).

The four actual people fictionalized as the novel's "quartet" were all creative people. Ford was the major-domo of Anglophone writers in Paris in the early twenties; Stella Bowen, his companion, was a painter; Jean Lenglet, Rhys's first husband, was a journalist and a writer, as was Rhys herself. But Marya, Stephan and Heidler are not writers: Marya is a former chorus girl but not a writer; Stephan a trader in art objects; and Heidler a "picture–dealer" (*Q*:6). This is a nicely ironical positioning in relation to Stephan – having more money, Heidler escapes the necessity to cut corners in what he buys and sells. Lois paints, as Bowen did, but it does not seem that this is very serious, given her commitment to Heidler's life in bars and her concern that she facilitate his young lovers. Stephan is literary, however: he tells Marya he took care of the prison library at the end of his sentence: "oh, my dear, *what* a selection of books!" (*Q*:135). There are other creative artists of various degrees of seriousness and accomplishment in the novel. These include Esther de Solla, a serious painter, the cabaret singer Cri-Cri, the former Ziegfried Folly, Plump Polly, members of a party Mr. Rolls the author gives at the Bal du Printemps, including a "little funny man, who is a sculptor" (*Q*:73) and Cairn, the American short-story writer. This being Paris in the twenties, there are also those whose artistry goes into creating themselves, via particularly theatrical and exact makeup or cross-dressing, as well as those whose art entertains others, like the violinist who has to play "sentimental music on muted strings" (*Q*:143), or the "something-or-other girls" who do acrobatics (Q:143), and those whose art is about amusing themselves privately, like the Japanese man who draws "elongated and gracefully perverse little women" on the tablecloth in a café (*Q*:140). There is also reference to fairs and circuses (Q:57) and marionettes (Q:105). Marya, letting others control her, is a "marionette," but she thinks Heidler is one too (Q:105). What this does is to heighten the reader's attention to the artistry of the novel, since its story is about the interaction of people who practice, appreciate or sell art.

The plot follows from the interaction of the major characters, like the unfolding of a drama. The four central characters make up two troubled couples, but then their relationships interchange as in a complicated board game. Marya is the central character because her relationships with the other three are crucial to the movement of the novel. She is married to Stephan but has an affair with Heidler and an understandably tense relationship with Heidler's wife Lois.

In the early stages of the novel, Rhys introduces all four characters via the kind of brief, particular physical descriptions that suggest character traits, similar to her method in describing Miss Bruce in the story "Illusion." Marya is blonde, "not very tall, slender-waisted," and she has a "short" face, "high cheek-boned, full-lipped; her long eyes slanted upwards towards the temples and were gentle and oddly remote in expression" (*Q*:5). As if attracted to her strangeness, "shabby youths" approach her to "speak in unknown and spitting tongues," presumably themselves foreigners (*Q*:5). Lois has "the voice of a well-educated young male" and she and her husband are "fresh, sturdy people" (*Q*:10). Heidler, who is "perhaps" forty-five, is tall, fair, with "tremendous" shoulders, an "arrogant" nose, and broad, dimpled, short hands (*Q*:11). He has intelligent light-blue eyes, but they have both obtuseness and even brutality. Lois is "plump and dark" (a description Rhys used in her story "Illusion") and her eyes are "beautiful, clearly brown, the long lashes curving upwards," but also suspicious and "deadened" (*Q*:11). Finally, when we meet Stephan, Marya thinks he looks very thin "after the well-fed Heidlers" (*Q*:13). She embraces him "violently" (*Q*:13), which suggests something is amiss. It is not until later that we see him as a "short, slim, supple young man of thirty-three or four, with very quick, bright brown eyes and an eager but secretive expression" (*Q*:17). His mind is described as "clean-cut" and "hard," but also as "disconcertingly and disquietingly skeptical" (*Q*:17). Each character is both appealing and subtly disturbing. That Heidler and Marya are described as obtuse/brutal and remote/gentle respectively suggests, as with the other main characters, that something problematic but harmless can easily combine or turn into something difficult or even dangerous, making what seems like an ordinary story of love gone wrong into a far more sinister tale.

The interactions of the major characters are therefore understandably complicated. Stephan's mind seems to appeal to Marya more than his body. She accepts (even enjoys) his criticism of her clothes and of her body: he thinks her arms are too thin and that she is a "Slav type" and needs petting (*Q*:8). He acts, oddly, both on impulse and "always in a careful and businesslike manner" (*Q*:18), which gives Marya both a sense of excitement and one of security. She lets him pay, and does not ask penetrating questions about his business dealings. Sometimes he goes away and leaves her alone in the hotel: she knows he is both secretive and a liar, but he is a good lover, and he treats her very well, as well as appealing to her by occasionally seeming like "a little boy" (*Q*:22). The same willingness to discard warning signs occurs when Marya notices how Heidler's uninvited hand lies on her knee "possessively, heavy as lead" (*Q*:13). She also cannot decide whether she likes "or intensely" dislikes Lois Heidler's touch, but acutely senses that Lois is most nervous when she sounds most firm (*Q*:48).

Though the four main characters are very different, they share traits. Marya and Heidler express their feelings at times in the same sort of melodramatic fashion, especially when alcohol is involved. Lois and Marya both listen at doors, despite Marya's denying that she would. Misunderstanding is rife also. Stephan misreads the Heidlers entirely. Heidler and Lois imagine Marya will tolerate their different abuses of her and give themselves praise because they are helping her. Marya underestimates the impact of her final cruel confession on Stephan, and too late sees the danger to herself she has caused.

By making both respectability *and* a naive admiration for those who break society's rules suspect, the reader is forced to withhold simple moral judgments. When Marya says she can't go on with the sexual relationship with Heidler whilst living with him and Lois, Heidler says she is "not playing the game" (in the British sense of playing by the right rules), and wants neither Lois nor himself to suffer public embarrassment if Marya goes "off in a hurry" (*Q*:89). Marya is dubious about the men Stephan has met in prison, who live by their wits and outside the law: they seem to lack any respectability and worry her, but she does not seem to take in the real impact of the changed Stephan who returns from confinement. Rather, she idealizes him as a "frail and shrunken apostle" (*Q*:133): the convicted thief is spiritually ennobled whereas the smug middle-class Heidler is the real thief of other people's happiness and opportunity. Yet Stephan has a gun when he meets Marya for the last time, though he does not threaten her. On his side, he says that *grues* (prostitutes) take care of their men. This is an ironical comment on Marya, who didn't take care of him, and became a kept woman with Heidler. He goes off, very unhappy, with an apparently warm-hearted if highly self-interested prostitute at the end.

Rhys carefully, if subtly, maps the chronology of the story, though the reader needs to pay close attention to decipher it. The novel begins in October, during the time Marya and Stephan are living in Paris after their marriage (*Q*:5). A year they recently spent in Brussels is mentioned in one abrupt sentence. What is more important is its lasting effect on Marya: she has accepted the unevenness of income Stephan provides and has ceased to suspect him. In the immediate shock of hearing Stephan is arrested, Marya notices the trees on the Boulevard Clichy stretch "ridiculously frail and naked arms to a sky without stars" (*Q*:26) Though the month is not mentioned, there are several references to weather typical of a Parisian October. The Seine reflects lights like jewels (it is five in the afternoon and clearly dark by then in mid-autumn; *Q*:29). When she goes to Lefranc's to see the Heidlers, she has a cold, it is raining, and she gets chilled. When Stefan is sentenced to a year in prison, we learn he will be free in September, so we know this takes place in October also. Other references to weather reinforce impending winter. Marya walks on the Boulevard Arago shortly after seeing Stephan in the Santé prison, and it is foggy, with a "cold sharpness in the air" (*Q*:46). She finds a bar on the Avenue D'Orléans for some coffee (she is cold).

The next spring comes early and "very suddenly" and Marya enjoys being in the Luxembourg Gardens and seeing the cosmopolitan crowd there (*Q*:67). It is on an unusually warm spring night, "a wonderfully still and brooding night," that Heidler makes his first unsuccessful move on her (*Q*:71). The next day is "cloudless, intoxicating" (*Q*:74). After Heidler seduces Marya, some time passes, and then at the end of April Marya's friend Cairn invites her to meet him, to find out what is happening to her.

After a dramatic scene at the Heidlers' country place in Brunoy in which Marya hits Heidler, she moves out of their place in Montparnasse. When Marya tells Stephan about this she also reminds him that he will be free in four months, so this is June. Through the summer, she continues a complicated relationship with the Heidlers. Heidler visits Marya in her hotel in an oppressively hot August (*Q*:127). Stephan is free "the second Sunday in September" (*Q*:125). Heidler finds her hotel too hot in September. He sends her to Cannes, which is hot, until "suddenly, the weather changed," and it is cold and grey (*Q*:164). Back in Paris, it is cold on a café terrace, as she tries to sort out her feelings for Stephan and Heidler, and it is a cool night when Stephan leaves her at the end of the novel. Thus the main action of the novel takes a little over a year.

The beginning of the story is structured like the opening act of a play. The last paragraph of Chapter 2 offers a comment on illusion replacing reality, important because it follows Marya's meeting Heidler and the description of her willingness to ask no probing questions when Stephan goes away mysteriously: both have to do with self-deception and Marya's capacity to dream. Then the plot moves along quickly in succeeding chapters: Stephan is arrested and jailed, accused of selling stolen paintings, leaving Marya alone and penniless. Marya falls into the clutches of the Heidlers and becomes their project, their neurotically desired source of drama and also self-praise, and finally, when she refuses to behave, their highly disliked problem. Stephan finally gets out of jail and discovers that both his trust in his wife and his appreciation of the Heidlers for helping her is misplaced. After Marya refuses to help him take physical revenge on Heidler, and then not only declares her love for Heidler but threatens to betray Stephan to the police, he becomes so enraged he pushes her away from him and she hits her head on the edge of the table. He leaves her unconscious (perhaps even dead).

Accident and coincidence play key roles in the action and outcome. Marya turns into a street after failing to find Esther de Solla to ask for help and sees the Heidlers walking together on the other side of it, but they do not see her. After moving in with them, Marya encounters Esther in the street and sees discomfort or disapproval in her face. Stephan runs into a female acquaintance just when he is in need of solace as the novel closes.

Rhys has other ways of engaging the adroit reader. Like T. S. Eliot, Joyce and Hemingway, she uses place evocatively, and to provide a richness of association that supplements the spareness of her prose. Eliot's "Little Gidding" evoked a real place, where a seventeenth-century Anglican community had lived in England; Hemingway's famous story "The Snows of Kilimanjaro" used the legendary Kenyan mountain as an active element in his story of the ending of a man's life.[8] The stories in *The Dubliners* collectively evoke Joyce's critical and complex reading of the city of Dublin. As in *The Left Bank*, Rhys uses Parisian geography very deliberately in *Quartet*, and the careful reader will find this is an important subtext in the novel, by which Rhys indicates aspects of the emotional, social and economic circumstances of her major characters.

We meet Marya first coming out of a café on the Boulevard du Montparnasse, the broad artery on the Left Bank that connects the Boulevard des Invalides with the Boulevard Port-Royal. She compares it to London's Tottenham Court Road, which immediately places it for British readers (the novel was published in London) as a bustling, cosmopolitan, bohemian thoroughfare. It is here and on Boulevard St. Michel (which runs between the Seine and Boulevard Montparnasse) that she has been accosted by "shabby youths." So we know she is here often. Her friend, the artist Esther De Solla, lives "in a street at the back of the Lion de Belfort" (Q:6), in Montparnasse. Marya is acutely aware of changes in the social fabric of the city's neighborhoods: she never wants to walk to the end of the Rue Vaugirard, because it is so respectable, preferring to go "far enough towards Grenelle" and then turn "down side streets" (Q:8). These details are easily located on a map of Paris.

Marya loves to find places where flamboyant and elegant cross-dressers hang out (Q:8), but Stephan highly disapproves of such adventures. Twice they have lived in a cheap Montmartre hotel, in the north of the city, far away from Marya's favorite haunts.[9] She first meets the Heidlers at Lefranc's, a small restaurant on the Boulevard du Montparnasse (Q:10), whose clientele is mainly English. At the end of the evening, Heidler puts her in a taxi to go back to Stephan and their hotel, which is quite far, across the Seine. She arrives after midnight in the Rue Cauchois, a little street not far from Boulevard de Clichy: Montmartre is later described as having "hazards" (Q:15). Not too far away is the Moulin Rouge, the infamous home of the can-can, and far more risqué and entertaining chorus girls than Marya had ever been.

Stephan has known Montmartre for fifteen years but seems to have made no strong personal connections there. From the balcony of their hotel, Marya can see the Place Blanche in one direction and the Rue Lepic in the other, which would certainly be possible from a hotel in the Rue Cauchois (Q:22–3). Lights from the Moulin Rouge shine as Marya goes out after hearing of Stephan's arrest. She comes out of the Métro into Montmartre at the Place Denfert-Rochereau. She then hurries to the Avenue d'Orléans, a part of the city where English is often heard. Her friend Esther's studio is close by, but she is not in. Marya then sees the Heidlers at a distance walking along the Rue Denfert-Rochereau. To find news of Stephan, she goes the next day to the Palais de Justice on the Quai des Orfévres, on the Île de la Cité which lies in the middle of the Seine (Q:29) She takes a taxi back to Montmartre (a ridiculously extravagant thing to do given her financial fragility). Finally, she finds out that Stephan is in the Santé prison, near the Métro station of Denfert-Rochereau, in Montparnasse. It is ironical that Marya's husband is confined in the district she so loves.

The prison is described as having an outside wall that "frowns down on the Boulevard Arago," which indeed is actually true (Q:35). Later Marya is late to meet the Heidlers at a restaurant on the Boulevard St. Michel, which is quite a walk (Q:47). Afterwards, Lois and Marya walk along St. Michel and cross over into the Avenue de l'Observatoire, which intersects with St. Michel and cuts across Denfert-Rochereau. The Heidlers live here, "halfway up the street." Stephan is moved to a prison in Fresnes and to visit him Marya must take a tram from Paris, from the Porte d'Orléans, the end of the Métro line south of Montparnasse.

Now Marya lives in Montparnasse, with the Heidlers, eats lunch each day at Lefranc's, travels to Fresnes each Saturday to visit Stephan, and, as a dependant in the Heidler household, runs errands at Lois's request, such as picking up a wig in the nearby Rue St. Honoré. She eats dinner alone in the Rue St. Jacques, just behind Denfert-Rochereau and close to the Heidlers' place, with a pitiful gesture of pride in spending her last hundred-franc note. Lois offers to get her a job as a mannequin in the Rue Royale (in an affluent district on the opposite bank of the Seine from Montmartre.) When the Heidlers leave for their place in the country at Brunoy, on the way to Fontainebleau, Marya stays at their apartment, and eats close by again in the Rue St. Jacques. She goes for walks, avoiding St. Michel and "its rows of glaring cafes," preferring the "Boulevard Montparnasse," "softer, more dimly lit, more kindly" (*Q*:67), where she can more easily dream. It is after one such evening that she meets Esther De Solla, outside a café.

There is a cartoonish gathering of artists in a scruffy little café on the Rue Mouffetard, not far from where the Heidlers live. Afterwards, Heidler makes a move on Marya in a bar quite close to where he lives with Lois. But the next day Marya escapes to meet with her friend Cairn in a restaurant on the Place Pigalle: by coming to Montmartre she has returned to the part of the city where she used to be happy with Stephan (*Q*:74). Then the Heidlers' apartment, Lefranc's, a music hall with naked girls, a bar in Montparnasse and Luxembourg Gardens all successively witness Marya's seduction by Heidler and its aftermath. Eventually she moves out of the Heidlers' apartment and goes to a seedy hotel that looks down on the Gare de Montparnasse. The name Hôtel du Bosphore has a vague and ironic overtone of tired exoticism (*Q*:110). Heidler takes her to eat at a restaurant called "Versailles" (also an ironical name), in the Rue de Rennes (not far from the hotel), but insists that she is seen at the apartment or at Lefrancs, so no-one thinks there is a quarrel. Marya takes to drinking alone, avoiding the Boulevard de Montparnasse and finding cheap restaurants where she will not run into the crowd around the Heidlers. Sometimes she takes walks and wanders into the very street where the Heidlers live. But on the seventh day (an ironical echo of Genesis), she "rests" from the Heidlers and visits Fresnes, once more Stephan's wife.

As Stephan comes close to being freed, Marya finds him a room in a cheap hotel in the Latin Quarter, but forgets his clothes are left in the hotel in Montmartre. After Heidler summons Marya and Stephan to a meeting, she abandons Stephan to get into a taxi with the Heidlers, to go to the Bosphore, only to announce on the way that she is going to go back to Stephan after all. She eats with him extravagantly in the Rue de l'Ecole de Médécine, just off Boulevard St. Michel, in the very territory that is associated with the Heidlers.[10] They go to the major train station, the Gare du Nord, not too far from where they used to live, from where he is to leave for Amsterdam. She continues in the taxi to Bosphore. After a difficult encounter with Heidler, she walks across the Place du Maine and up "the avenue," presumably the Avenue du Maine, to find a place to drink and lose herself. Despite her initial resistance, she does take Heidler's suggestion, and funding, to go to Cannes, and then visits Nice. Stephan calls her back to Paris to meet him when he returns and gets a room for her in a hotel near the Gare du Nord (*Q*:160). This is an area with old happy memories for Stephan and Marya. Then after their final quarrel, in the spare room of his friend Bernadet, Stephan goes off to somewhere near the Gare de Lyon, from where he will leave France. Clearly Rhys mapped this geography very carefully, and realizing it adds greatly to the reader's apprehension of the novel.

Rhys represents a range of ethnicities, which signify the cosmopolitan nature of a great city. Many characters are migrants (not only the primary four, but also Marya's one-night stand, whose family live in Toulon and are immigrants from Tonkin). Stephan is Polish. Esther de Solla is Jewish (and resistant to the English), as is one of the men Stephan was in prison with. Stephan comments, "People abuse Jews, but sometimes they help you when nobody else will" (*Q*:137). "Michel the nigger" is another former prison-mate of Stephan's (*Q*:135). Marya's face is described by Heidler as "Kalmuck" (a term for Mongol people), in the same moment that he calls her "savage," just before they have sex (*Q*:131). When Stephan and Marya go to a bar, there are Chinese students dancing there, as well as a "little flat-faced Japanese" drawing on the tablecloth. These references make clear that Marya and Stephan are part of a cosmopolitan city, in which the "Anglo-Saxons," like Heidler or Cairn, are one of the most privileged groups of foreigners. Marya is separated from the English in Paris by her exotic looks and her attitude: she is described as "a Slav type" by Stephan early in their relationship. Marya sees Heidler as German (which is a negative). When she wants to hurt him and is very angry, she calls him "Horrible German" (*Q*:104). Mademoiselle Simone Chardin, who goes off with Stephan at the end of the novel, is "swarthy" and has curly hair, perhaps suggesting she is of mixed race.

Then alcohol, a significant agent in the late-Romantic artistic circles in 1920s Paris, significantly drives the plot. Marya only realizes that the drawings Esther de Solla shows her are beautiful because of alcohol (*Q*:6). Many of the locales in the novel serve alcohol. Marya and Stephan drink white wine with ice cubes in it when they cannot afford food, because wine makes the world seem different, more tolerable. After Stephan's arrest, Heidler fills up Marya's wine glass constantly (we therefore assume she is emptying it frequently too; *Q*:40). A Miss Lola Hewitt is moody, and Lois prescribes another brandy. At one of Lois's parties, two male guests fight because a woman who sculpts complains to one about the other: alcohol is not mentioned but seems a likely element in the story. Everybody is somewhat drunk by midnight at parties that Marya enjoys. Heidler is drunk when he tells Marya he is obsessed with her. Cairn invites her to have a cocktail at lunch (they do drink coffee afterwards; *Q*:74) and on another occasion he drinks gin and vermouth whilst he writes to invite Marya for lunch (at which they drink burgundy; *Q*:91). Even sin is equated to a drink, for Heidler, when he says to Marya in church that we are all sinners, more or less, "a dirty glass or a very dirty glass" (*Q*:95). When the Heidlers take Marya to Brunoy, Lois drinks more than usual at dinner, then leaves Heidler and Marya together. Heidler claims to be "awfully drunk" after Marya confronts him and Lois over their treatment of her: he says he will not remember anything of this in the morning, which Lois affirms as a habitual ploy (*Q*:104).

Marya imagines women lying in the bed she occupies in the Hôtel du Bosphore, "crying if they were drunk enough" (*Q*:119), enough to endure loveless sex and also know it. When lonely, Marya drinks the very strong Pernod, "to deaden the hurt" (*Q*:121), though she is sternly advised not to do so by a kindly, if interfering *patronne*. Stephan has been in jail and thus not able to have alcohol for a year, and he wants to go to a bar the first night she meets him after he is free. When they meet the Heidlers, Stephan unsuccessfully tries to prevent Marya drinking brandy, which triggers her rejection of him. After Stephan leaves Paris for Amsterdam, Marya meets Heidler and he orders them both coffee and brandy, as if he controls her tastes and desires. Marya drinks brandy alone after Heidler makes it clear she is to "go down South" on his money and "get well": the affair is over (*Q*:150). She goes with a stranger that night, evidently for a sexual encounter. In Cannes, she drinks a lot of Pernod alone (a very bad sign) after she has a disturbing visit from a friend of Lois. This bender (together with taking veronal) makes her very sick, and she badly bites her own arm in her drugged state (*Q*:161).

When Stephan comes back to Paris illegally, he orders four Pernods for himself, Marya and his host and partner. Marya drinks a second round of this with the two men. There is a third round, after which Marya and Stephan eat a cheap dinner, wine included: the last we see of them, they are visiting Stephan's friend Bernadet, who the next day finds Marya where they drink aperitifs. Afterwards, she blames the alcohol (which she continues to drink after Bernadet leaves) for making her feel so empathic towards Stephan's vulnerability and hurt: ironically she therefore leaves half the glass. When she meets Stephan next he has wine and rum to go with a cold meal. He drinks rum after hearing her confession of the affair with Heidler, and then threatens to hurt Heidler, even showing a revolver he carries. Every time alcohol is mentioned, it is a specific drink that has a specific effect (all of them are ruinous, of course, if consumed to excess). The choice and number of drinks mark particular emotional choices and conditions, especially in Marya.

Marya also smokes (*Q*:5), as so many did in the 1920s, when smoking became fashionable for bohemian women as well as men. Heidler complains she smokes too much (*Q*:78) and Stephan is annoyed that she breaks up a cigarette on his bed after he comes out of prison (*Q*:137). There are other drugs. A "fresh-faced boy" says he can drink anything and "pull myself together in a minute" (*Q*:42), and gives Marya something in a capsule that evidently increases her heart-rate and makes her flush. Like Djuna Barnes, Rhys depicts a fast life lived on the edge, but each brutally realistic detail of drug use is functional in the plot.

This was Rhys's first attempt at full-length fiction and in it she worked out how to integrate all the elements of her style and her thematic concerns with great economy. Both the plot and the visual intensity of Rhys's writing lend themselves to the cinematic. Though she would use similar techniques and even thematic elements again in her work, each of her texts also has its own unique texture, and though some critics have seen her protagonists as the same woman in different locations, each one has a particular identity.

After Leaving Mr. MacKenzie (1931)

If *Quartet* is structured like an elaborate emotional chess game, Rhys's second novel seems to be structured like a three-act play. It has three sections (like three acts), subdivided into numbered and titled chapters, which may be seen as dramatic "scenes." Two innovations are introduced: the chapters have titles, and the sections are numbered instead of being separated by asterisks. As in the case of *Quartet*, these are then often subdivided. Part I has four sections, subdivided into 5, 7, 4 and 3 subsections respectively, Part II has 14 (subdivided 2, 2, 2, 4, 4, 3, 2, 3, 7, 6, 3, 3, 2, 3) and Part III has 3 (subdivided 3, 2, with the last one not subdivided at all). The plot is laid out like a well-made play, with an opening "act" to set up the plot and characters, a substantial central "act" which complicates and deepens characters and their dramatic interaction, and a third "act" to resolve the action and bring it to a close. The emotional tone is both comic (often bitterly ironical) and tragic (in the sense of the crises that change lives in major ways being connected to personality, a version of the idea that character is fate. Ellipses are again important in this complicatedly structured novel: scene shifts are sometimes dependent on dialogue for the reader to fully realize them, which gives a sense of eavesdropping on impulsive characters who change direction on a whim. They also provide for shifts in narrative point of view, from Julia to MacKenzie, Horsfield, James and Norah and back.

There are scenes with a great deal of dialogue, such as in the chapter "Mr. Horsfield." Rhys includes references to both literature and film. At the time the novel is set, literature provided ideas for thinking about life for the middle class: Conrad's *Almayer's Folly* offers Julia's sister Norah a depressing comment on the emotional numbness of a trapped slave, which she both associates with herself and then resists (*ALMM*:103).[11] Uncle Griffiths talks of Dostoievsky.[12] But the film is on its way to becoming mass entertainment. Julia dislikes plays, which she finds "unreal," and prefers films, falling into the illusion that filmed representations of fictive characters are more "real" than characters portrayed by actual human beings in the theater, moving and speaking in real time (*ALMM*:133). She and Mr. Horsfield go to the cinema.

As in *Quartet*, Rhys pays attention to geography. The thirteen chapter titles indicate either places or locations like a staircase. This is a tale of two cities, London and Paris. These two cities are contrasted in three of her five novels. In this case, Part I is set in Paris, Part II in London and Part III in Paris. When the novel opens, Julia Martin lives on the Seine waterfront, in a cheap hotel on the Quai des Grands Augustins, opposite the Île de la Cité, the location of the Palais de Justice. She likes to lunch at a German restaurant in the Rue Huchette, very close to the street in which she lives. This section sets up her habits and inner emotional landscape by tracking her through locales (something Rhys began to do with regard to her central character in *Quartet*). She goes to her former lover's house, walking along the Boulevard St. Michel. Standing outside in the dark she sees him come out and walk towards the Boulevard Montparnasse. She follows. Part I ends with Julia being approached by a strange man near a dark quay on the Seine, opposite the Île de la Cité, and then leaving Paris for Calais, on her way to London.

The second "Act" concerns what happens in London: chapters are titled Acton, Golders Green, Notting Hill (and then one mocks this specificity, "It Might Have Happened Anywhere"). Julia goes to a hotel in Bloomsbury, close to a similar location she had left "nearly ten years before" (*ALMM*:67). Bloomsbury of course is known for its famous literary and intellectual associations, most notably because of the presence of the British Museum, London University and the "Bloomsbury Group" around Virginia and Leonard Woolf, their friends and her extended family and their friends, during the first quarter of the twentieth century.[13] It is thus parallel in many ways to the Left Bank, but the Bloomsbury Group is upper-class and well-heeled, unlike Julia. She passes a man selling violets on the corner of Woburn Square, walks into Tottenham Court Road, crosses Oxford Street into Charing Cross Road, gets lost in Soho, and goes back to Oxford Street, an easily achievable walk and one familiar to any London reader. Julia's uncle lives in Bayswater, appropriate for a shabby-genteel man: after a difficult meeting with him, she gets on a bus "going in the direction of Oxford Circus" to meet Mr. Horsfield (*ALMM*:86). After dinner they cross Regent Street to find a place to have a drink. Julia's mother and sister live in Acton, in the suburbs west of the city. Julia moves to a boarding house in Notting Hill. Like Bayswater, Notting Hill is to the north of Holland Park and the northwest of Hyde Park, not in central London. We do not learn the address of either Mr. Horsfield or Julia's rich ex-lover, Mr. James, but James's house is clearly an impressive town house and Horsfield's (to which Julia never goes) is quite unnerving, "quiet and not without dignity . . . part of a world . . . of passions, like Japanese dwarf trees, suppressed for many generations" (*ALMM*:175). She goes by bus to see a film in the Edgware Road, also well outside central London. Mr. Horsfield promised to find her a better place than the hotel in Bloomsbury, but he seems a frugal sort of man, and Notting Hill is likely at the time to have offered cheaper accommodation. Her mother's cremation requires the family to take hired cars to transport them to Golders Green, a well-known crematorium established in 1902, where the ashes of famous people have been scattered. It is a significant distance from Acton, to the north of Hampstead. Later Horsfield and Julia go out in her neighborhood, though he thinks snobbishly the place where they finish their evening "was more to be expected in the provinces or in a very distant suburb" (*ALMM*:146). He would have preferred to go to the famous Café Royal, in the centre of London, long associated with famous writers such as Oscar Wilde, Aubrey Beardsley and George Bernard Shaw, Stephen Spender and Dylan Thomas.[14] After Julia's landlady sees him sneaking up the stairs to her room, he thinks he ought to get her a room in "Paddington or obscurer Bloomsbury" (*ALMM*:169), which would not be too expensive for him and would give him more anonymity, not being his sort of area of London.

In the third "Act," Julia is back in the same part of Paris as she was in Part I (as if it were the same stage set). Her hotel overlooks a square in the Île de la Cité. She goes for a walk and sits on a stone seat "near the statue of Henry IV on the Pont Neuf," which connects the western end of the Île de la Cité to both banks of the Seine (*ALMM*:181), and walks along the Quai des Orfèvres, on the Left Bank side of the island. She decides to shop in the Avenue de l'Opéra, just north of the Louvre, in an affluent district on the opposite side of the river. After dinner, she walks along the Seine, in different directions (towards the Place St. Michel, the Place du Châtelet, and finally Les Halles, known for the famous market. Mr. Mackenzie is having a drink in the Rue Dauphine, which runs south of the Pont Neuf.

The chapters are titled as if in a nineteenth-century novel, charting the moral journey of a protagonist (such as a woman fallen from grace through her own weakness and the demon sex). Rhys puts a different, ironical spin on that genre by exposing the ordinary, depressing vacancy that lies in the center of much of what we call sexual passion or love. She also switches narrative point of view from time to time to include both male and other female perspectives.

Chapter 2 is titled "Mr. Mackenzie," a significant former lover, from whom Julia receives a letter containing a cheque he announces is the last one he will send. Chapter 3 is titled "Mr. Horsfield," who becomes a new man in Julia's life. Chapter 4, "The First Unknown," refers to a man who tries to pick her up as a prostitute on the street. Part II begins with "Return to London," identifying a geographical location just as the first chapter of Part I did in the title "The Hotel on the Quay." The second chapter, "Norah," is a dramatic interaction between Julia and Norah, her sister. "Uncle Griffiths" follows, about Julia's attempt to get money from this disapproving relative.

Both of these chapters see the world from Julia's point of view, but the fourth chapter, titled with the name of the café where she accosts Mr. MacKenzie, witnesses Horsfield's struggle with himself over his attraction to Julia. "Acton" is the location of Julia's difficult reconnection with her family, and the narrative focus switches in mid-chapter to Julia's sister Norah. "Mr. James" is another former lover (the Mr. or gentlemanly titles for all three men are deliciously ironical). Chapter 7 is "Change of Address," to signify Julia is now living in Notting Hill. "Death" is that of her mother and "Golders Green" the cremation, though it includes the lunch afterwards back in Acton. "Notting Hill" is about her journey back from Acton, her encounter with a man who tries to pick her up, and an evening with Horsfield. The ironical title "It Might Have Been Anywhere" is about the sexual encounter between Julia and Horsfield.

The next chapter, "Childhood," is Julia's escape from the present and her attraction for Horsfield, who says "you've given me back my youth" (*ALMM*:161). In "The Staircase" he comes back for another sexual encounter which involves creeping into the house, only to be thwarted by the landlady. "Departure" finds Julia packing to go back to Paris, having been evicted from her room the next day, and leaving Horsfield, who is still attracted but relieved. The opening chapter of Part III is titled "Île de la Cité," again indicating something of importance to Julia will happen here. "The Second Unknown" is another strange man, very young, who follows her until he sees her clearly under a street lamp. The last chapter is, appropriately, called "Last."

There is a great deal of structural detail in this short novel. Over and above the chapter structure and the geographical detail, Rhys repeats the motif of three (three lovers or ex-lovers all titled Mr., and three strange men who approach Julia). Throughout, the motif of money connected to sex is evident. MacKenzie, Horsfield and James all give Julia money to make themselves feel better. MacKenzie is flustered enough by the request she makes at the end of the novel that he sticks a bundle of currency into her hand, probably more than she has asked for. Horsfield feels "powerful and dominant" the first time he gives her cash (*ALMM*:47). Money raises their hopes that her unacceptable behavior after they have had their way with her will go away if she has money to spend. The only time Julia thinks about earning money from a job is when she writes an advertisement in Paris in which she optimistically describes herself as a "*jeune dame*" of thirty-six, speaking French, English and German, and seeking to be a companion or a governess (*ALMM*:180). Rhys locates the price (and therefore class) level of eating places and bars carefully. Julia eats twice at a Lyons tea-shop, a popular low-cost chain of restaurants at the time, so we know she is a bit short of cash, because she usually likes interesting, bohemian places. Twice when she gets money from a man she spends it on clothes (first second-hand, the other time new), so we know she prefers instant gratification and looking good in public to stretching out the pennies.

Alcohol plays an important role once more. Like Marya, Julia drinks, both wine and strong drinks, like Pernod in Paris. Rhys gives the detail that she drinks it at times without enough water, which is a bad sign. Julia follows and accosts Mr. Mackenzie one evening after drinking Pernod, responds to Horsfield after brandy, and after more drinks agrees to go to a film with him. After that, he takes Julia to his hotel and they drink whisky and soda. The next time she sees him they begin with sherry, drink something else with dinner, then have liqueurs, and then Julia has a brandy and Horsfield a whisky. That evening ends, unsurprisingly, with him recoiling from the smell of brandy on her breath. The next time they meet, they have wine with dinner, and then Julia wants an after-dinner brandy but there is none available: that is the night they first have sex. Julia is "bewildered, sleepy," "soft and unresisting" (*ALMM*:153) and impossible for Horsfield to fathom emotionally: perhaps she has had enough drink to make her woozy but not enough to make her belligerent. On the last evening together in London, Julia drinks most of a bottle of wine and is then quite hostile to him. Back in Paris, she drinks wine at lunch, then three brandies after dinner, all in different places, before two Pernods with Mr. MacKenzie. Julia drinks alone in public. She drinks in private in her room. She drinks with the men she wants to impress and have as her protectors. She gets drunk, and then her voice changes and she becomes "passionate and incoherent" (*ALMM*:42). She reflects that striped wallpaper makes "her head ache more when she awoke after she had been drinking" (*ALMM*:10). A landlady is reported as minding the bottle Julia brings home each night more than the chance of her coming home with a man. Drinking makes the Seine seem like the sea to her. After a solitary dinner one night (where she probably had something alcoholic to drink), she finds her anger at MacKenzie for stopping payments to her comes out at the man who seizes her arm and wants to buy sex from her: she wants to hit him but is afraid he will retaliate. It is also clear that Horsfield's most sympathetic responses to Julia are fueled largely by alcohol.

Rhys makes the alcohol dependency functional in the novel, for it explains Julia's strange moodiness, and her willingness to go along with what men want. But she does sometimes seem to experience genuine emotions without the mask of alcohol when with her family. The reader does not know if alcohol is drunk at the lunch after the cremation, but Julia is aggressively emotional with her sister and, tellingly, Norah thinks Julia is talking in an "incoherent voice" (*ALMM*:135).

Emotional immaturity clearly contributes to the family drama. There are many references to adults as if they are babies or young children in the novel: Julia's mother cries like a child, Julia appears to look at Horsfield "like a baby" (*ALMM*:40), but thinks her attempt to get money from her uncle is "childish" (*ALMM*:84), the stranger who accosts her in Paris turns out to be "a boy" (*ALMM*:187), and Julia remembers she originally left England because of a feeling she thinks a boy might have, wanting to run away to sea (*ALMM*:51). Mr. James's handwriting is "rather like a boy's" (*ALMM*:172). Julia's family is dysfunctional, made up of two estranged sisters who nevertheless have some tormented affection for each other as well as the dying mother and a chilly uncle. There is no mention of a father. Julia is said to have lost a child in an early marriage that took her away from England immediately after the First World War ended. This is of course what happened to Rhys. Horsfield finds it easy to imagine Julia as a child (*ALMM*:161). Even if Julia's emotions are intense in response to her family, they are more genuine and less confused: "a dam inside her head burst, and she leant her arms on her head and sobbed" (*ALMM*:130).

But once again, the plot is not the most important aspect of this novel. There are, as in *Quartet*, images and themes that provide key subtexts. One is around the arts, most especially the visual arts, but also music and literature. In the tawdry room Julia stays in at the beginning of the novel, there is "fantasy" wallpaper, with a large bird facing a half-lizard, half-bird, sitting on a strangely ornate branch, and a faded pink imitation satin cover on the bed, suggesting tawdry sex (*ALMM*:10). There is also an unframed still-life in oils which suggests a painter needed to settle his bill by leaving his work. The still-life (of a half-empty bottle of wine and some cheese) and the red plush sofa strike her as the idea and the act, presumably of sordid sensuality: she sees them both as having "perversion."[15] A picture in a shop window depicts a man "encircled by what appeared to be a huge mauve corkscrew" (*ALMM*:15), the colour mauve a key clue to this comic representation of modernism's distortions of reality. Julia talks about a Modigliani painting of a woman lying on a couch, "with a lovely, lovely body . . . like an utterly lovely proud animal" (*ALMM*:52). Her face is like a mask but Julia finds as she looks at it more, it seems as if she is looking "at a real woman, a live woman" (*ALMM*:52). The reserved and pompous Neil James collects pictures, which he loves, and which seem to make him "a different man" (*ALMM*:115). Julia once was an artist's model and a mannequin, and it is clear that she regards clothes and makeup as the essential props that can give her a place in the world. Men will do things for women they regard as beautiful (thus Julia worries, with poignant clarity, about the way men see her as losing her youthful attractiveness). Women who are clearly trying to be appealing to men but who have lost their looks are taken for prostitutes.

But it is not sex that is key here. The sexual scene with Horsfield shows Julia to be emotionally remote. Sex is a means by which to acquire protection and economic support, and to give an illusion of not being alone. The three English lovers each have significant emotional damage, and are easily turned off women, or to put it another way seem to choose women with whom they cannot have a long-term comfortable relationship, so justifying their constant withdrawals. For them, art and emotions have complicated interactions. James finds buying art is the safe place where he can let his affections free; for Horsfield, an enjoyable "illusion of art" comes when he is sitting with Julia in a cinema, somewhere a little out of his own world ("that bare place," with "frail music"; (*ALMM*:44)); and for Mackenzie, emotional mistakes are somehow connected to the poetry he wrote in his youth.

Money is a substitute for affection: the men may offer cheques in the mail to make up for their inability to give or receive love. The only way a woman can make herself feel independent or virtuous is to refuse the money (or refuse casual sex). Thus ageing is a very worrying development. For Julia and Norah, mirrors are both friends and enemies, in which they search for affirmation of their surviving looks or for the cruel truth that they are no longer young enough to capture male attention. A terrifying old woman, with a "white face and black nails," malevolent eyes and a "cringing manner" (*ALMM*:14, 15) reminds Julia of the horrible possibilities that may lie ahead. So a hat with a veil can act as a mask or shield that keeps the world away. A room is also a shelter from public gaze. These change as an income diminishes (rooms in hotels give way to rooms in boarding houses). But those rooms can also be prisons, self-imposed or as the result of not having the resources to go out into the world and do what is interesting and distracting.

Creatures, both real and fantastic, are again important. Both Norah and Julia call people they do not like "beasts" (*ALMM*:104, 135), though Norah retracts this. Julia also thinks "animals are better than we are" (*ALMM*:135). Julia and her "second unknown," the "boy," are "tense, like two animals" (*ALMM*:187). Julia's landlady early in the novel thinks that Julia lives "the life of a dog" (*ALMM*:11). Julia knows she hasn't "a dog's chance" against a rich man and a lawyer working together against her (*ALMM*:22): there is a "doggy page" in an English newspaper she reads on the boat-train coming back to London (*ALMM*: 61). Miss Wyatt, who helps Norah take care of her sick mother, has an alert expression, like a terrier (a feisty little dog with a sense of purpose; *ALMM*: 97). A woman Julia sees as "mournful and lost" is "like a dog without a master" (*ALMM*: 145). Master is a term applied to Horsfield in relation to his cat, with whom he seems to have as close a relationship as he is capable of with anything or anyone, though it quickly becomes inconvenient if the cat doesn't get out of his way. The cat is also odd. It *gallops* to meet him as if it were a dog, but it has "rather malevolent eyes" (*ALMM*:168), just like the old woman Julia sees whose eyes are the last evidence of a negative emotion that is keeping her alive, and her mother in her last days, whose eyes seem more animal than human. Ironies abound, as in depiction of dead lobsters and birds painted on the walls of the restaurant to which Julia goes to with Horsfield, "ready to be eaten" (signifying the reduction of living creatures to food in the most crude way; *ALMM*:144). The memories of childhood which occupy Julia just after the desolate sex with Horsfield involve butterflies, a child's thoughtless catching of them and breaking of their bodies. The ending of the novel has to be read in the light of these references: "It was the hour between dog and wolf" (*ALMM*:191). Julia has been dog and is becoming wolf.

The statement about dog and wolf is connected to twilight, the transition between light and dark. This novel is filled with oppositions and transitions such as cold and warmth, dreams and nightmares, fear and happiness, death and life, ghosts and the living, hardness and softness, tragedy and comedy.

Whatever is in the outside world (political and social pressures) or inner emotional space is deferred to and absorbed into these large generic oppositions. Sometimes Rhys makes an unusual juxtaposition, as when lights are hard.

Tiny details are again important, often repeated. Flowers (especially red roses) reflect conventional emotional responses (the extravagant red roses that Julia takes to her mother, bought out of the little money she has left, the small artificial red rose Norah wears on the shoulder of her dress, sewn on, reflecting her lack of a love life).

Julia is sensitive to the shape of particular things, including houses that are alike: "Each house she passed was exactly like the last. Each house bulged forward a little. And before each a flight of four or five steps led up to a portico supported by two fat pillars" (*ALMM*:85). This gives an exact idea of Julia's dislike for the smug gentility and self-protectiveness of houses that belong to the materially affluent with aspirations to social prominence. She also rejects a fat man who approaches her 'and' strongly dislikes her own appearance after she has put on weight. Rhys's use of such tiny details and also of heightened sound patterns is reminiscent of poetry. Flowers (such as red roses) reflect conventional emotional responses: Julia spends more than she can afford on them for her mother, and Norah's small artificial red rose, sewn on the shoulder of her dress, indicates her lack of a love life, or of passionate emotions. Rhys's economical prose is often made the more poetic by the use of alliteration and assonance. In the following passage, s (and sh) are prevalent, counterpointed by other less obvious repetitions of consonants such as f: "Julia stared at the bed and saw her mother's body – a huge, shapeless mass under the sheets and blankets – and her mother's face against the white-frilled pillow" (*ALMM*:97). There is a distinct rhythm to this sentence, made the more noticeable by the use of pauses. Sometimes Rhys employs alliteration to heighten a description made rhythmic by two or three nouns or adjectives connected by "and" ("short and slim"), or by several multisyllabic words in a passage made up mainly of monosyllabic ones: "He leaned forward and stared at her, and she looked back at him in a heavy, bewildered, sleepy way" (*ALMM*:153). The final shift to the monosyllabic "way" is effective in conveying the fuzzy, complicated expression she has at this moment.

Rhys's second novel has some important commonalities in detail with her first. The names of the protagonists are rhythmically similar: *Ma*rya *Ze*lli, *Ju*lia *Ma*rtin. Bold wallpaper disturbs the protagonists (such designs were popular in the 1920s and 1930s). The word "chic" is important in both texts. Pairs of colors mark particular emotions: in both novels pink and red signify sex, but in *After Leaving Mr. Mackenzie* red and green are associated with Norah's suppressed sexuality and attempt to be a pure woman, and colors are minimal (and often faded): dark, black, white, pale and gray predominate. Dark is particularly key in Julia's emotional lexicon, applied to buildings, streets, people and clothing (pale is also important). Juxtaposing dark and pale recalls black and white films. Even people are often thus described: "very pale and with very small, dark eyes" (*ALMM*:187), "white face" (*ALMM*:155), "her face was dark and still" (*ALMM*:74). Clocks signify in both novels: the protagonists have no set routine or employment or stable emotional ties and so paradoxically time exists as a painful reminder of what they are not doing right. Also, just as Marya has oriental eyes, Julia has oriental hands: both signify they are slightly exotic to the European men who are attracted to them.

The plots of both novels have clear connections to events in Rhys's own life, so making them have distinct similarities in detail if not in overall movement (the men in *After Leaving Mr. Mackenzie* are deliberately vaguely drawn, however, and quite similar). Both Marya and Julia are capable of self-destruction and careless of their health and well-being. Gender is a minefield for a woman in both novels, where traps and dangerous hidden threats lurk under the surface everywhere and men feel free to stereotype women and avoid looking hard at themselves. Fatigue haunts both Marya and Julia (emotional as much as physical). But Julia has none of the hopes and dreams of Marya: their different ages and the fact that Julia is more deeply emotionally damaged than Marya mark them as very different women. It is very clear that in this second novel Rhys was settling into her novelistic practice: her highly structured text withholds any comfort for the reader. It has an atmosphere reminiscent of Eliot, particularly of *The Waste Land* (1922): "My nerves are bad to-night. Yes, bad. Stay with me."[16]

Voyage in the Dark (1934)

This novel is a *bildungsroman*, a novel about coming of age. Often this is a first novel, but for Rhys it comes third. It may be that Rhys needed to wait until she had two well-constructed novels behind her before mining some of the material in her first unpublished attempt at a novel, "Triple Sec."[17] This time, the story is about a very young woman, Anna Morgan, and the love affair that causes her great emotional and ultimately physical damage. As in her previous fiction, Rhys does not attempt to contextualize the story in the public events of the novel's chronological moment, in this case the onset of World War I.

Voyage in the Dark was published in the middle of the 1930s, the period of stressful and widespread economic hardship following the First World War, which may have contributed to Constable's editor, Michael Sadleir, asking for the ending to be changed to something more positive. Critics have been divided as to which ending is the stronger: Rhys evidently did not choose her original manuscript ending to replace the first published one when the novel was reprinted after many years.

The irony is that, whereas the revised ending satisfied Sadleir, it isn't really positive at all, and can still be read as a subtle suggestion that Anna's spirit and will to live are broken. It is tempting to find Sadleir's insistence on changing the ending as a typically male bid for control over a female author's work. But the longer ending indulges Anna's nostalgia for her childhood and betrays Rhys's own stern rule of tight control and ruthless cutting to keep the shape of a text. The rambling memories are vivid and interesting but ultimately place far too much emphasis on Anna's loss of home, with a real danger of sentimentality arising from leaving the reader with a final image of her as victim. They plunge the reader into the prison of Anna's fading consciousness, ending with a final descent into an implied death. Also the longer ending has references to the deaths of both Anna's parents, whereas the revised ending makes the novel focus more on Anna's father's death, which reverberates effectively with Walter as surrogate father-figure (though horrifically careless and exploitative). There is a passage early in the novel when Anna is sick with some sort of flu, which is very similar in tone to the original ending (the ramblings of a mind unable through ill-health to bring coherence or rationality to the expression of memory and feelings). It is the more effective to have just one such passage in this fairly short text. There is also a fuller description of Carnival in the longer ending, with a great deal about masks, as well as references to earlier parts of Anna's story, namely her affair with Walter, but this material doesn't add anything to the novel of sufficient importance to prefer the longer ending.

The original ending clearly utilized parts of Rhys's notebooks (specifically the Red). When the ending was changed, she was free to use what she had excised for other texts. Her unfinished autobiography, *Smile Please* (published posthumously in 1979) begins from the professional photographer who takes a picture of the young Rhys. This passage was the opening for the original version of the last section of *Voyage in the Dark*, showing how Rhys cut and pasted material and then reworked it to suit the fictional purpose at hand. There is a character called Meta in the original ending also, a servant who evidently loved Anna's mother as well as being stern and provoking the young Anna. But in the autobiography Meta is only the cruel and frightening nurse.

The "dark" in *Voyage in the Dark* reverberates strongly in the novel. It is metaphoric for Anna as well as real. When Anna lies in bed haunted by the fact that she has become a bad girl, the kept woman of an older man, she thinks this makes no sense but that "something about the darkness of the streets" does have a meaning (*V*:57). She wants the lights out when she and Walter have sex (*V*:56). Though dark is a key word in much of Rhys's fiction, here it has a particular emphasis because of the juxtaposition of Anna's romantically remembered brightly colored Caribbean and the absence of bright colors in England (except on one bright summer day when Anna goes with Walter to Savernake Forest). Walter wants to have adventurous sex in the forest in public (he is anonymous there), but strictly brought up Anna thinks that sex has to be behind a closed door, with curtains over the windows. Sex and darkness are closely associated for her.

This novel has four parts, but there is no contents page, unlike in *After Leaving Mr. Mackenzie*, announcing the structure and substructure (in this *Voyage in the Dark* is like *Quartet*). There are once more subsections to each of the four parts (asymmetrical in number, respectively, 7, 5; 7,1). The subsections are numbered as in the case of *After Leaving Mr. Mackenzie*, but there are no chapter titles. The first part is long (a hundred pages, telling the story of Anna's whole affair with Walter). In Part Two, Anna meets the "masseuse" Ethel, half-heartedly begins to associate with call-girl Laurie and her clients, then moves in with Ethel. Part Three is the period at Ethel's, and then Anna's move to stay with Laurie, who arranges Anna's abortion. Part Four is the aftermath of the abortion.

Anna has much more of a youthful energy than either Marya or Julia. Marya's "air of fatigue, disillusion and extreme youth" (*Q*:18) which Stephan Zelli notices when he first meets her, is never attributed to any experience she has had but is clearly a symptom of emotional dysfunction. Julia Martin is even more severely damaged (among other things she knows "(i)t was always places that she thought of, not people"; *ALMM*:12). But Anna Morgan is a little cheeky and wayward, an attractive, spunky girl making her own way in a hard world. Rhys chose first-person narration for this novel and so needed a central character whose consciousness is appealing (and complex) enough for the reader to sustain attachment to her story. In *After Leaving Mr. Mackenzie*, all the major characters are emotional losers, but here Rhys constructs the voice of a girl who is a genuine ancestor of Antiguan writer Jamaica Kincaid's feisty female protagonists.[18]

Anna is a chorus girl in England when we meet her. She misses home, in the West Indies. But she isn't at all the cliché of the mindless young hoofer. She likes to read, and, shortly after the beginning of the novel, she is reading

Emile Zola's *Nana* (this is a very subtle connection to the major role of France in Rhys's own life, and in that of female protagonists in her first two novels).[19] First-person narrative provides opportunity for the reader to engage with the senses of the narrator, the power of smell, sight and touch. Smell is a powerful agent in personal memory for Anna, for the smells are so radically different in England that she feels the connection between things and identity is "different." At the cinema with a new friend, Ethel Matthews, she says it "smelt of poor people" (*V*:107). The flat of her call-girl friend Laurie "smelt of her scent" (*V*:114). An older man, d'Adhémar, wears scent, which makes Anna feel queasy (affirming that she is pregnant).[20]

She also has a subversive sense of humor in the beginning which is far more effective for being heard directly through the first-person voice. She has evidently learned much from her fellow chorus girls, such as Maudie, about the way working-class girls have to learn to deal with the world of exploitative men. Maudie's cockney accent is confident: when she meets a man whose clothes and accent suggest he has money and is therefore of a higher class, and he ignores her request for his name, she says, "I was speaking to you, 'Orace. You 'eard. You ain't got clorf ears" (*V*:12). On Anna's first evening with Walter, a dinner in a private, oppressively decorated dining room, she can't help seeing the similarity of his face (especially his nose) to the waiter's: "The Brothers Slick and Slack, the Brothers Pushmeofftheearth" (*V*:20). She describes a disliked landlady as having a face "like a prawn" (*V*:103). The reader is entertained by her subversive response to powerful older figures around her and knows other characters in the novel are not in Anna's confidence.

But there is gradually more and more anger under Anna's voice. Like Marya and Julia, she becomes capable of violence towards a man who has used and abandoned her. But whereas Marya hits Heidler and Julia slaps Mackenzie across the face with her glove, Anna presses a lit cigarette hard into Walter's hand after he laughs at her in a particularly insensitive way (*V*:86), showing she is not just a young and innocent victim. It gives him another reason to end the affair. Though they have sex afterwards, he dismisses her apology for the injury to his hand and smoothly talks about his unavailability to see her before he goes to New York (a trip about which he never told her). Her anger has no one focus after Walter's abandonment of the relationship. She describes a policeman as staring at her "like a damned baboon" (*V*:148). She tells Ethel, the seedy masseuse, that it is "damned funny" that her client scalds his foot. She brings a man back to Ethel's place, gets drunk, throws a shoe at a picture of a "damned dog" and thinks of the man as "(t)he fool"(*V*:161). First-person narrative gives Rhys the chance to convey the dislocation between public face and private thoughts, and the total lack of productive introspection in Anna.

Anna's sense of the world dominates the novel. The rather stagey homesick paragraph that locates the island in which Anna was born alongside a description of it as "all crumpled into hills and mountains" (a reference to an anecdote about Columbus's description of Dominica) leads into a memory of arriving in England with her stepmother Hester.[21] Rhys gives Anna's stream of consciousness the same kind of breathless flow of feelings and thoughts that characterize her own notebooks, in which she withheld punctuation, did not complete sentences, and included repetition as reinforcement of an idea. Anna's internal narrative is similarly constructed: "smaller meaner everything is never mind – this is London – hundreds thousands of white people white people rushing along" (*V*:17).

Rhys's story is also enhanced by the use of letters, folk stories and by reference to well-known literary works. As in the earlier novels, letters are key. Rhys wrote most of her work in the era when people could receive a letter and send a reply by return of post, making letters the key bearers of good and bad news as well as agents of misunderstandings. Modes of telling folk stories in the West Indies are also important, and remind us that Anna is *talking* to us, for the voice changes depending on how she is feeling.[22] There are few scribal literary references but they are significant. Apart from Zola's *Nana*, which Anna reads, an unattributed line from Coleridge's "Kubla Khan" is part of Anna's experience of a film she goes to with Ethel (*V*:107).[23] Vincent has read and enjoyed *The Rosary* and so assumes it is written by a man, but Walter points out it is written by a woman, exposing Vincent's extreme gender prejudice (*V*:85). Anna thinks of a frightening story about walls getting smaller in a room to crush someone, "*The Iron Shroud*, it was called. It wasn't Poe's story" (*V*:30). Teresa O'Connor identified "The Iron Shroud" as a terrifying story by William Mudford, about a man being slowly crushed to death in a prison cell whose walls move in[24] and *The Rosary* (1904) as written by Florence Barclay. O'Connor says it "sentimentally extols the virtues of "Christian womanhood".[25] As elsewhere in Rhys's work, popular songs are important, such as "Adieu, sweetheart, adieu" (*V*:22), "Connais-tu le pays" (*V*:161, 162), "By the Blue Alsatian Mountains I Watch and Wait Always". (*V*:162), and "Camptown Racecourse" (*V*:152, 154–5).

Art is significant here as elsewhere in Rhys's work. Some of this is popular, the kind of cheap reproduction sold for hanging in rented rooms, like "Cries of London" (*V*:139, 179), "Cherry Ripe" (*V*:44), a picture of a little girl fondling a dog, "Loyal Heart," the dog sitting up begging, at which Anna eventually throws her shoe (*V*:148, 161); and some of this is expensive, like the paintings Walter Jeffries collects (he also has a "damn bust of Voltaire," as Anna terms it; (*V*:87).[26] Wallpaper is a key detail in *Quartet* and *After Leaving Mr. Mackenzie.* In *Voyage in the Dark* it is only mentioned once, vaguely: Ethel's sitting room has white wallpaper with stripes. Music is particularly important in the novel, appropriately since Anna is a chorus girl who lives in the world of music hall, where working-class culture enjoys both escapist fantasies and tongue-in-cheek social commentary. West Indian culture is also indicated here, including references to folk beliefs (the *soucriant*), story-telling practices and obeah, as well as religious terms associated with Catholicism, which is strong in Dominica (hell, damnation, devils).[27]

This is Rhys's portrait of the destruction of hopeful youth by a web of emotionally dysfunctional people, most centrally Walter. Anna is young twice over, chronologically and because of her childlike emotional nature. When Walter Jeffries first meets her, he thinks she is younger than her age (eighteen). This is a sinister detail, because he goes on to enquire if Hester Morgan is her mother, and finds out the girl has only a stepmother, who he may assume will not directly protect her (*V*:15). He knows she was born in the West Indies, about which he, like most of his countrymen, probably has assumptions that will not work in Anna's favour. Maudie is a bit older than Anna, but she is also much wiser than her years, and she calls Anna "kid" (*V*:45). Walter describes his young friend Vincent as "a good-looking boy" (*V*:49), but Vincent becomes his agent in dealing with Anna when Walter wants to distance himself. The summer after the novel begins Anna is nineteen. Vincent still calls Anna "the child" and "infantile Anna" (*V*:80), says Walter has been "baby-snatching" (*V*:85), and that she will be "a great girl one day," addresses her as "(m)y dear child" (*V*:87), and, in the letter telling her the relationship with Walter is over, calls her "nice girl" and "dear Infant" (*V*:93). In their final meeting, he calls her "(p)oor little Anna" and "(m)y dear girl" (*V*:172, 173). Walter called her "only a baby" when he first seduced her (*V*:51) and, later, "you rum child" (*V*:55). Vincent's friend Germaine says Anna is "awfully young" (*V*:85). One of Anna's landladies calls her "a young girl" (*V*:90) and another a "young lady" (*V*:106). Ethel says Anna seems "well under twenty" (*V*:112) and both Ethel and Joe, a man who wants to seduce Anna, call her "kid" (*V*:155, 156, 125), though when Anna's call-girl friend Laurie tells him she is not seventeen, Joe challenges that, thinking she is older. The woman who does the abortion speaks to Anna "as if she were talking to a child" (*V*:177). But this "child" is seduced by Walter, loses her good name, and sinks into an increasingly sordid life of casual sex for money, culminating in the abortion that almost causes her death.

Like a child, Anna apprehends the world through simple opposites – warm and cold, sad and happy. When Walter first touches her hand, she is cold (she is always cold in England). When he first tries to seduce her, she feels cold, despite a fire in the bedroom. The next time, she feels "fire" until he talks about her being a virgin, and then she is cold, until she gets into bed with him and his body is warm and she wants the warmth. She does not adapt to England but remains emotionally frozen as the child she was in the Caribbean, shown by her simplistic but urgent expression of the difference between England and the Caribbean: "a difference in the way I was frightened and the way I was happy" (*V*:7); "how sad the sun can be . . . but in a different way from the sadness of cold places" (*V*:56). Her apprehension of emotion remains simplistic throughout the novel: "it was sad" (*V*:57, 74), "being afraid is cold like ice" (*V*:88), "cold as life" (*V*:154). Anna remembers the Caribbean in vivid colors, such as gold, red, blue, green and purple, as well as "fire-colour"; England is pale and gloomy and emotionally frigid.

Anna was formed in a racially divided culture. We know she has absorbed racist white cultural norms by the way she speaks: "the narrow street smelt of niggers" (*V*:7); "the black women" (*V*:7) carry fishcakes to sell on trays on their heads. "The" objectifies them. She also remembers her childhood desire to be black, which entirely misses the realities of the racial hierarchy in which she is privileged and expresses itself in terms of warm and cold again: "being black is warm and gay, being white is cold and sad" (*V*:31). In a sense, when she is called "the Hottentot" by the other chorus girls, she is given a "black" identity. Their casually picked up, unquestioned English racism fuses Anna with the sexualization of African women (made into a lurid sensation when the "Hottentot Venus," Sarah Bartmann or Saat-Jee, was on view in London in 1810, from whence this association bled into popular culture).[28]

Clearly a binary structure was Rhys's intention, as we can read from her original title "Two Tunes".[29] Many details juxtapose opposites. In England, Anna is conscious of "white people" and "dark houses" (*V*:17). When Anna finds poems in a drawer in her rented room in London, left by a bad poet who lived there before, she mockingly reads out some lines to Maudie, "*But where are they – / The cool arms, white as alabaster*" (*V*:47). Her childhood memories represent race as performed by whites. She was raised to be a white "lady," forced to wear a woolen vest, starched drawers, petticoat and dress, black wool stockings and brown kid gloves to church in the tropical heat, and then live up to an expectation that ladies do not perspire (*V*:41–2). A Miss Jackson Anna knew as a child stayed out of the sun to protect her "dead-white face" (*V*:162–3) because she was "Colonel Jackson's illegitimate daughter" (*V*:162), and so probably of mixed race. She was educated and gave French lessons, but being caught between the races meant she lived a lonely life.

Yet Anna's fondest memories suggest that she breached racial divisions somewhat. She remembers a Venezuelan girl and Black Pappy, her family's boatman, fondly, but a white policeman is a "fair baboon . . . worse than a dark one every time" (*V*:148). Her stepmother Hester was nervous about racial categories not being properly enacted as different: "never seeing a white face from one week's end to the other and you growing up more like a nigger every day" (*V*:62). Hester hears Anna's Uncle Bo as having "exactly the laugh of a negro" (*V*:65), and that "(e)xactly like a nigger you talked" (*V*:65). Hester wanted to send away Francine, the servant girl who was close to Anna, and refers to people of color as "these people" (*V*:68). But Anna also objectifies race in her casual conversation, still a colonial child in a racist society. Hester has two "jumbie-beads" from the Caribbean which are set in gold as a brooch: she plans to give this to a rector's daughter who is getting married. She wants to check with Anna that the "niggers" say such beads are lucky: the way Anna replies "Yes, they do . . . They always say that" (*V*:58) implies she is an authority, but doesn't belong to "they." Anna thinks about the Caribs not intermarrying "with the negroes" at home (*V*:105). When talking about how Francine did not know how old she was, she says, "Sometimes they don't" (*V*:68). Anna knew Francine did not like her because she was white.

As in other Rhys texts, a number of ethnicities are present, demonstrating in small but telling details the complex hierarchies of English class and race prejudices of the early twentieth century. White Creole women, were imagined to be highly emotionally volatile, over-sexed, and fond of the bottle. When Anna meets a man to whom she mentions that she was born in the West Indies, he jokes about this, claiming he knows Trinidad, Cuba, Jamaica. Then he stereotypes the Welsh as heavy drinkers (Morgan like Rhys is a Welsh name), saying he knew her father: "Taffy Morgan . . . didn't he lift the elbow too" (*V*:125). Anna is very conscious of who might be Jewish. She buys clothes from the Misses Cohen, she asks Maudie if her man Viv is a Jew, and Maudie responds quickly, "Of course he isn't" (*V*:16), suggesting the pervasive casual anti-Semitism of English culture at the time. Anna thinks Joe is "very Jewish-looking. You would have known he was a Jew wherever you saw him, but I wasn't sure about Carl" (*V*:113). Clearly locating every individual with regard to ethnic or racial origin is a part of Anna's world in England, the still very imperial, hierarchical, self-defining racially homogenous culture of the early twentieth century.

The novel's representation of sex is chilling. When Anna reads *Nana*, we have no sense that she realizes that Zola is trying to portray the existence of a prostitute, but Maudie knows "it's about a tart," and likely to be full of lies, since it is written by a man (*V*:10). Anna's fantasies about race are also deeply intertwined with her sexual role-playing for Walter. She tells Walter that she always wanted to be black as a child (*V*:52), and that she remembers seeing old slave lists, with the name of Maillotte Boyd, an eighteen-year-old house slave. Walter's response to her memories is that he doesn't like hot places. There is a moment at their first private meeting when Walter admires Anna's teeth, recalling the way planters looked at slaves. During sex Anna imagines being dead, lying stiffly with her arms by her side and her eyes shut. She asks for the light to be out. Then she thinks of Maillotte Boyd. The words that follow, "*But I like it like this. I don't want it any other way but this*" (*V*:56), suggest Walter has sex with her as if she is a commodity, in the way the master would have had sex with the slave. He comments afterwards that she lay so still he thought she was asleep, something Anna thinks of as the after-sex moment called "*the Little Death*" (*V*:56), after orgasm. But the conflation of a young slave girl with Anna Morgan, the descendant of the slave owner, is troubling, suggesting how deep and problematic Anna's fantasies run.

References to performance link the chorus-girl experience of Anna with her childhood witness of Carnival. Related to this are references to disguises and costumes (masks, makeup, hair dye). But sometimes gender signals are ambiguous. Vincent has "curled-up eyelashes like a girl's" (*V*:80). Class is also a performance, managed through the semiotics of clothes, such as Laurie's squirrel coat, or the distinctly up-market coat, dress and hat that Anna buys with Walter's money from the Misses Cohen on Shaftesbury Avenue in London, who sell clothing with an "insolence that was only a mask" (*V*:27). But the irony is that the good clothes, which Anna wears back to her rented room, are spotted by her landlady as proof positive that she is a prostitute or a kept woman. The landlady is working class, but she claims superior status as a respectable woman: "I don't want no tarts in my house" (*V*:30). This is the second working-class landlady to respond negatively to Anna and her chorus-girl friends. The first was in Southsea, where "good rooms" went along with the landlady at first saying "I don't let to professionals," invoking the old association between girls on the stage and prostitutes, and later on demanding that the girls not come downstairs unless they are "decent," that is, respectably dressed. Respectability must be properly performed.

The role of sex in the story is also linked to role-playing. Early in the affair with Anna, Walter chillingly mentions her "predecessor" as "certainly born knowing her way about," which lets the reader know Anna has no future with him (*V*:51). He is generous but cautious (he hails a taxi in the street near his house in the middle of the night so that no-one will know who he is or where he lives). Anna hopes for love, but her fellow chorus girls know sex and youth are a tool a woman can use for only so long, hopefully to snag a husband, a piece of real estate, or, at the least, a good fur coat. It is a short distance from that to Laurie's work as a call-girl: she is quite clear about the separation of profitable sex and love. But Walter at times confuses them for Anna (one of his letters says "I love you so much"), and she is young enough to believe him. Thus, for Anna, sex is about becoming protected, loved and cherished. On the basis of Walter's apparent affection, she drops out of the chorus (and therefore her only steady income). But then he pulls back into his protected life.

This novel's chronology is very precise. It begins in October, when Anna meets Walter. Her birthday is in January, on a Sunday, a day when Walter is never in town (*V*:40). Hester comes to London on February 1 and again in mid-March. At the height of a hot summer, Walter pulls away. At the beginning of October Anna gets the devastating letter from Vincent, telling her that it would be better if she didn't see Walter "just now." By November (which is unusually warm), Anna has been associating with Laurie, and then moves in with Ethel. A letter from Ethel to Laurie complaining about Anna is dated March 26, 1914. Anna is pregnant and, according to Ethel, three months gone, and the novel ends with the aftermath of the abortion.

Geography signifies once more. Though Anna's memories of Dominica are for the most part less specific in terms of precise locations (though she does mention Market Street and the Bay), the houses Rhys knew as a child are evoked in detail. The house in which Anna Morgan grew up is described as in much the same place in relation to the sea as Rhys's own childhood home in Roseau. The house Rhys grew up in in Roseau is still there, and is clearly the basis for Anna's childhood home, with its upstairs bedrooms with the jalousies, the stable-yard, the garden with a huge mango tree and a damp bathroom with a large stone bath. Constance Estate, with the ruins of an old house surrounded by a garden run wild, recalls Rhys's mother's family property of Geneva. Morgan's Rest, with a favorite hammock on the verandah and a view of the ocean, resembles Rhys's father's holiday house of Bona Vista.

Within two pages of the opening, Anna's memory of Roseau (and the sea) is juxtaposed with memories of the English coastal town of Southsea. We know her island is Dominica partly because of the longitude and latitude provided, and also because she eventually names Dominican "mountains," such as Morne Diablatin. There is general reference to streets and theaters in seaside resorts like Southsea and Eastbourne where Anna's touring company performs. Anna meets Walter in Southsea (raising the question of what a rich gentleman like Walter was doing on "the front" (the walkway looking onto the beach). Maybe he is slumming, looking for working-class girls. Hester lives in Yorkshire but travels to London for sales, showing she knows how to make the most of her money as well as enjoying it. She has relatives in Cambridge which may suggest a connection to the intellectual upper middle class. Walter takes Anna out of the city by car during the summer to Savernake. Anna breaks her unhappiness over him by going to Minehead for three weeks, which is far from London, on the north coast of Somerset.

But London is where most of the present-time action occurs. Anna takes a room in Judd Street just before her first dinner with Walter. This is a main street near Euston and St. Pancras stations, marking the need for economy. The chorus girls' hostel (the "Cats' Home") is in Maple Street, not far away, off Tottenham Court Road. The restaurant where Walter first takes her is in Hanover Square, near Soho, a colorful and cosmopolitan area. When Walter gives her money, she goes to Shaftesbury Avenue to shop, in the heart of the expensive West End, near Piccadilly Circus. Walter's house is in Green Street, in the most affluent and exclusive part of London, Mayfair, near Park Lane. Anna moves to Adelaide Road, not far from Chalk Farm tube station, after her landlady evicts her. This runs between Camden Town and Swiss Cottage, to the north of central London, but not so far away that she could not get to and from Walter's house. Hester stays in Bayswater, signifying her shabby-genteel status (like that of Uncle Griffiths in *After Leaving Mr. Mackenzie*). In the summer, Anna goes to Primrose Hill (an extension of Regent's Park). A wonderful view of central London can be seen from there and it is also near an area associated with a number of famous writers, including W. B. Yeats, Friedrich Engels and H. G. Wells. It is also quite close to Camden, where Anna lives. When Walter returns to London from his overseas trip, they meet at a hotel in Marylebone Road, near Regent's Park, at his suggestion: it is equidistant from both of the places where they live, and therefore neutral ground. Anna changes addresses partly to stop Walter from knowing where she is, but stays in Camden Town, which is where she and Ethel go to see a film together. Ethel lives in Bird Street, and Rhys adds the detail, "just off Oxford Street, at the back of Selfridges," (the famous department store), right in the heart of central London (*V*:111–12).

Asked to get out of her rented room so it can be cleaned, Anna goes to Tottenham Court Road tube station and along Oxford Street, where she runs into Laurie, who lives on Berners Street, not far from Oxford Circus. She and Ethel both ply their trade in an area of high commercial traffic of all kinds, where a man can be anonymous. After an evening out, Laurie's client Carl goes off by himself to Clarges Street, to the southern end of Mayfair. This reference is no further explained, but is an area where an upscale club could have been located. The men Laurie knows can also rent rooms in hotels where the staff turn a blind eye to girls they bring in for sex. However, it is a different story for women: when Anna has a quarrel with Ethel she is tempted to go to a hotel in Berners Street but knows she will not be allowed to book a room without luggage (*V*:147). When she moves in with Laurie after leaving Ethel's flat, Anna tells Vincent she has found another place in Langham Street, not far from Regent Street, still in central London: Walter will pay for this "(v)ery swanky" place (*V*:179). In one of Walter's old letters is an invitation for Anna to be in a taxi "at the corner of Hay Hill and Dover Street at eleven" (*V*:174). This is right at the southern end of Mayfair, where Walter could collect her without having her come to his house, and that was even at the height of his attraction to her. So geography is just as key in this text as it was in Rhys's earlier fiction: it had become a deliberate and effective part of her fictional strategy.

There are many connections with the other novels, so much so that it is helpful to think of Rhys's fiction as like a series of long poems, each different, but requiring the reader to remember other texts to fully understand the individual identity of each one. Once again, there are many ellipses and filmic scene shifts. Mirrors are once more key, as when Anna walks into the bedroom off the private dining room on her first evening with Walter to find that her reflection in a "looking-glass" makes her feel that she is "looking at somebody else" (*V*:23). She stares at this image for a long time, making us aware of her immature narcissism (though each of Rhys's protagonists looks into mirrors with her own individual hopes or fears). When Anna goes to spend Walter's money on new clothes, there are two long mirrors in the shop. When she looks at herself in her lovely new outfit, she sees that her face looks "small and frightened" (*V*:28). A little later, Anna finds the streets look different, "just as a reflection in the looking-glass is different from the real thing" (*V*:29). She mentions twice how much she dislikes the mirror in Walter's bedroom, because it makes her look "so thin and pale" (an ominous detail; *V*:40). There are a few references to prison and confinement, recalling *Quartet*, but only to mark this novel's different mood. The sea is important in Anna's memories of Dominica, whereas the sea-coast or rivers are important elements in the first two novels. In this novel, animal images are few and confined to dogs: Vincent calls Walter a "dirty dog" for his relationship with the much younger Anna (*V*:86), and dogs are closely associated with the England Anna so dislikes. Even as a child she told her stepmother

Hester that she hated dogs, but Hester warned her that to say that in England would make people strongly dislike her (*V*:71).

Alcohol once more plays a key role, first as enabler and then as emotional anaesthetic for Anna. It is clearly a socially acceptable element in British culture, of whatever class. Maudie and Anna share port with Walter and his friend (and he refills Anna's glass). Walter questions the quality of a bottle of wine to impress her as he prepares to seduce her. They have two bottles of wine followed by a liqueur: Anna refuses both a second liqueur and sex. When he brings her nurturing food because she is sick, he also brings a bottle of burgundy. Anna is weak after being ill but thinks she sees the streets "as if I were drunk" (*V*: 35). After the first sex with Walter, in the middle of the night, she asks for a whisky and soda – Walter suggests she "have some more wine" instead so we know they were drinking earlier in the evening (*V*:38). On another evening, she tells Walter how liking drink too much runs in her family, and eventually realizes the whisky is fueling her stories about her childhood, to which Walter listens with some politeness and encouragement but not much interest. He does notice she is getting usefully drunk and it is time to go upstairs: he finds "champagne and whisky is a great mixture" – presumably for getting young women into bed. But much of the time Anna is happy with him alcohol isn't mentioned. As stress creeps in, on an outing outside London, Walter orders whisky and sodas for them for lunch. Once Walter leaves her, she turns to drink.

We see her at the outset of Part Two with a whole bottle of vermouth and a soda siphon (then she drinks the vermouth without the soda). Visiting the room of Ethel, who lives on the floor above, Anna asks for a drink and Ethel gives them both gin: gin makes Anna sick so she can't touch it at first but later she drinks it and it makes everything "seem rather comical" (*V*:111). Later another friend, Laurie, invites her for a drink (whiskies and sodas). Again, when she goes out with Laurie and two men, they drink Chateau d'Yquem and liqueurs, and Anna gets drunk. When they go on to a hotel, with one of the men who rents two rooms, there are more whiskies and sodas. Anna gets nauseous, and fails to have the expected sex. She finally moves in with Ethel, who greets her with plebeian bread, cheese and Guinness beer. On a slow day, Ethel drinks whisky and soda, becoming an enabler of Anna's drinking. Carl, who becomes Anna's casual lover, notices the effects and asks if she has been taking ether or something, "because your eyes look like it." Ethel leaves two bottles of champagne visible for the use of Carl and Anna when they come back to the flat to have sex. Then there are other men, but as long as there are drinks, "it was better."

During one drunken session, Anna suddenly feels sick. It is the clear sign of pregnancy. Even then, visiting an artistic friend of Laurie's, she has wine, and is offered brandy as well. She drinks (whisky and soda) with Walter's nephew Vincent from whom she hopes to receive money for an abortion. Brandy is given to Anna before the abortion (which induces a later miscarriage). When the miscarriage comes Anna asks for gin, despite Laurie thinking she should have champagne. The alcohol makes sexual experience bearable but emotionally inert, and also brings Anna's rage to the surface and removes her inhibitions about expressing it. Rhys again is a master at conveying the influence of alcohol on Anna and other characters.

As in earlier fiction, the protagonist has strained relations with her family: this time through bereavement and its consequences. Anna remembers both parents with love, though her affection for her mother has to be inferred from her love of Constance Estate, her "mother's family's place," which sounds as if Rhys based it on Geneva, the beautiful estate her mother's family owned.[30] Anna's mother is clearly a faint memory, and her planter father a strong one. The main family drama in this novel revolves around inheritance. Anna tells Walter that, when Hester married her father, he sold a larger country estate and eventually bought a smaller one. Hester has a voice that Anna hears as saying, "I'm a lady . . . I'm an English gentlewoman. I have my doubts about you" (*V*:57). Hester wants Anna to go back to the protection of Uncle Ramsay (Bo), and proposes to pay half her passage (to which Uncle Ramsay responds "where's the other half going to come from?" – *V*:60). Ramsay accuses Hester of having taken Anna's inheritance (a house that her father bought when he married Hester, sold after his death, called Morgan's Rest). But Hester argues that Anna's father paid too much for it and it was sold for far less than he paid, and that she has a small income and cannot afford to maintain Anna. Walter is both first lover and ironic father-figure, twenty years older, and therefore a potential provider. Though the first evening does not go well, Anna later likes him because he is kind when she is ill and gives her food and money. But Maudie worries he might be "the cautious sort" (*V*:45), which is not a good sign. When he tries to push Anna into taking her theatrical career seriously through his and Vincent's help, it is a self-interested mockery of fatherly protection: he betrays Anna the "child." There is also another seductive "father," d'Adhémar, called "Daddy" teasingly by Laurie. He speaks French, just as does one of the lovers Anna imagines in her semi-conscious rambling at the end of the novel.

Voyage in the Dark, like *Wide Sargasso Sea*, has little excuse to play English and French against each other, unlike the novels set in Paris, but there are moments when Rhys's characteristic multilingual fictional world manifests itself. Maudie speaks in a cockney accent, just as Francine speaks in Dominican patois. Mrs Robinson, the abortionist, is Swiss-French. Rhys does not translate the few French sentences she speaks. Germaine, Vincent's girlfriend, is half-French and lives in France, and has decided views on the failings of English men, quoting a Frenchman who said "there were pretty girls in England, but very few pretty women" (*V*:81), because "most Englishmen don't care a damn about women" (*V*:82). Anna remembers her father's house in Dominica and the way "the grass on the crête was burnt brown by the sun (*V*: 69): a subtle opposition of her own affiliation to the majority French Creole culture of Dominica as opposed to her stepmother's colonial English identity.

Rhys went on in her next novel to construct an extremely complex multilingual world, in which language is both functional and entirely meaningless by turns.

Good Morning, Midnight (1939)

This novel is her masterpiece, mordantly funny and at times highly satirical, very stylized and brilliantly observed, but it has generally been far less noticed and definitely far less loved than her two novels of tragic love for young women, *Voyage in the Dark* and *Wide Sargasso Sea*. This is not a story with immediate appeal: *Good Morning, Midnight* is about a woman falling into self-destructive middle age, and abandoning even the will to survive. The ending is emotionally heightened, as is true of all of Rhys's fiction, but whereas *Quartet* had a disturbing and even somewhat melodramatic ending, *After Leaving Mr. Mackenzie*'s close predicted future emotional crisis for Julia, and *Voyage in the Dark* concluded tragically and with unconvincing hope, *Good Morning, Midnight* leaves the reader simply shocked and even terrified. This is Rhys's bleakest novel, bleak as the year in which it appeared, 1939, when the Second World War broke out. Sasha, the first-person narrator, is also far more challenging to comprehend than previous Rhys protagonists, although she is amusing and intellectually interesting.

There is less plot in *Good Morning, Midnight* than in any other of Rhys's novels. Sasha wanders Paris, notices people and things, meets strangers, goes back to her rented room, shops, eats, and drinks: ordinary activities. But she is often reminded of her past. Even with minimal plotting, Rhys clearly found her previous experience in structuring novels had served her well, because this novel is once again carefully divided and subdivided. There are four parts, as in *Voyage in the Dark*, divided into unnumbered subsections demarcated by a large asterisk: further divisions are indicated just by a gap in the text. This is organized very much like *Quartet.* The four parts, respectively, have 81, 28, 36 and 42 pages, divided into 9, 2, 15 and 5 subsections: there is no pattern to the number of subsections in each narrative, but rather they are driven by the nature of the part of the story being told. The first and longest part sees Sasha settling into her stay in Paris and meeting a gigolo; in the second she reaches out to the artistic Russians Delmar and Serge; in the third, made up of many short memories, she tells the story of her early marriage to Enno; and the fourth builds inexorably to the devastating ending. Parts One and Two begin in the present, but go back and forth between present and past; Part Three goes back to the past; and Part Four stays in the present. Even when Sasha goes back to the past, the present tense is dominant in her telling of her story and this gives the narrative an urgent immediacy. Not everyone thought all this worked: one reviewer in 1939 commented that the novel was so "very modish" as to be "already out of date"[31]. But *Good Morning, Midnight* has lasted well, and now, in our postmodern age, Sasha's elaborately disrupted consciousness is not at all dated.

Though Rhys once again repeats certain motifs and stylistic elements from her previous work, the new note here is a sustained mordant irony. Irony is a particularly effective weapon for those denied social power or authority, and forced to conform on the surface to the expectations and orders of those who rule them: it is an important tool for postcolonial writers. Rhys made it her own in this text.

"Good Morning, Midnight" is the first line of an untitled poem by Emily Dickinson.[32] The first half of the poem is printed at the beginning of Rhys's text, so no reader can fail to recognize the novel's title (and Rhys would naturally expect the reader to look for and read the whole poem). It is one of Dickinson's most chillingly playful poems, the parable of a "little Girl" who complains that the Day she loves "got tired of Me – How could I – of Him." So though Midnight is "not so fair," she appeals to be taken in by him. Rhys's protagonist is, then, to be read alongside the pitiful choice of Dickinson's persona, and the reader is thus warned from the outset that this novel is likely to have a bleak emotional landscape.

The protagonist is self-named Sasha (her given name is Sophie, which conjures up a pretty, amenable character, something Sasha is not). This first-person voice is very different from that of the young Anna: Sasha is ageing badly and has tried to kill herself with drink. Rhys wrote that *Voyage in the Dark* was written "almost entirely in words of one syllable. Like a kitten mewing perhaps" (*L*:24), to capture Anna's emotional immaturity. Sasha is neither attractive nor admirable, and has not matured well, but she is Rhys's only intellectual, writerly protagonist. She tells René, the gigolo, that she is "no use to anybody" because she is a "*cérébrale*" (*GMM*:161), a thinker. She imagines a hilarious book titled "Just a Cérébrale or You Can't Stop Me From Dreaming," but, to be believed, it would have to be written by a man. René thinks this is "rather stupid," because he judges that she feels better than she thinks. For him a *cérébrale* "is a woman who doesn't like men or need them" (nor women either), and "likes nothing and nobody except herself and her own damned brain or what she thinks is her brain" (*GMM*:162). Sasha immediately links the reception of a woman trying to be intellectual to the attempt of an exploited child to please his oppressors: "So pleased with herself, like a little black boy in a top hat" (*GMM*:162). For Sasha, gender and race are closely connected, both deeply about exploitation.

In short, Sasha is too clever by half, and lives in a pre-feminist world in which women are still confined within many stereotypes and conventions. She is unfulfilled, a very female talent trapped in an old fur coat, and she has a much more developed self-scrutiny than Rhys's other protagonists. She lives in the 1930s, when women were supposed to gain social standing through marriage to a man (preferably of means), or, if they remained single, to hold onto respectability even in hard times. The solicitor who writes cheques to her as the income from a legacy asks her why she did not drown herself in the Seine (*GMM*:42).

As a character, she neither appealed to the pre-feminist reader (in 1939) nor, in her refusal to stop hurting herself, to the feminist reader (in the 1960s and 1970s), but she seems very much in tune with our postfeminist, post-modern time. In Sasha, Rhys offers an uncomfortable insight into the damage endured by people treated with contempt not only by those in power but by those ordinarily middle-class people capable of taking good care of themselves. Sasha is the first to see her failures clearly and cruelly, and yet she never loses her ability to strike out with thoughtful aggression against those who would destroy her. She is Rhys's most brilliant and chilling creation, because she demonstrates what actually happens to people who are not able to be the fittest who survive in a Darwinian world: Rhys herself was enormously strong through all manner of crises because she worked at her writing constantly. She withholds the bedrock of hard work from Sasha, source of sanity and satisfaction for Rhys herself. Though Sasha does have great skill with words, her only paid work as a writer has been to ghost for a talentless rich woman. The way she uses, thinks about and responds to language is the core of the novel. Sasha can sound absurdist. In absurdist literature (important after the Second World War but with roots in earlier aesthetic movements such as Dada and expressionism in the 1930s), language can sound perfectly meaningful at the level of the sentence but there is a disconnection between language and action.[33] Furthermore, Rhys seems to uncannily predict postmodernism's recognition of the inability of language to have stable meaning. Sasha struggles to communicate and, more than any other of Rhys's protagonists, lives in a multilingual world in which at times no language makes sense.

The young Sasha, a receptionist in Paris, needs to prove her multiple language skills to the London manager, Mr. Blank. But she even denies that she knows French well. She thinks, "when I am a bit drunk and am talking to someone I like and know, I speak French very fluently indeed (*GMM*:20). Then she finds she can't remember the "little German" she knows. So she hilariously imagines a speech of disconnected German phrases that tail off into absolute nonsense, such as the musical scale, "doh ré mi fah soh la ti doh" (*GMM*:24). Then she misreads his instruction to her about an errand because of his terrible French accent which makes "*caisse*" (cashier) sound like "kise" which she cannot fathom. So in revenge she silently composes a highly ironical speech to him. She immediately knows he thinks she is "inefficient . . . slow in the uptake . . . slightly damaged in the fray," therefore of little market value, which gives him the right to exploit and harass her, even to the extent of "this mystical right to cut my legs off." But she denies him "the right to ridicule me afterwards because I am a cripple" (*GMM*:29). This is one of Rhys's most powerful indictments of the rich and powerful whose money comes from systematically denying the humanity of others, even to the extent of slavery. Sasha says, "Every word I say has chains round its ankles; every thought I think is weighted with heavy weights" (*GMM*:106).

On another occasion, Sasha overhears the *patron*, *patronne* and two maids in her hotel having a conversation in French with friends. This consists of repeated phrases and sentences, "Tu n'oses pas . . . je n'ose pas? . . . Tu vas voir si je n'ose pas" (You don't dare, I don't dare? You will see if I don't dare; *GMM*:36). The pointless repetitive jollity marks their complicity and community and Sasha as outsider. When the painter Serge speaks to his Russian compatriot Delmar, Sasha thinks he "says something in Russian. At least, I suppose it's Russian" (*GMM*:98). She teaches English to Russian clients (so she should know something of what Russian sounds like).

Rhys's use of stream of consciousness in this novel is far more complex than in *Voyage in the Dark* because Sasha is older, more worldly and more intellectual than Anna. Sasha's memory is bound to be impacted by her many years of heavy drinking. She lives a great deal in the past, but her often vivid memories are scattered. From the opening paragraph, she is mercilessly frank but also highly unreliable and her story is convoluted. Even more than in her earlier fiction, Rhys confronts the reader with an impossible choice: identify with the dysfunctional protagonist, and her substance abuse, sexual promiscuousness and emotional dysfunction, or take the side of Sasha's respectable enemies, and become the mouthpiece of that culpable smug middle-class world that Sasha exposes.

Moreover, the reader must work at compiling a coherent narrative for Sasha as her memories take her back and forth in time, especially as she drinks too much and too often. Like other Rhys protagonists, Sasha is clear-sighted about her addiction. She thinks she can use alcohol to remove herself from time: "I shan't know whether it's yesterday, today or tomorrow" (*GMM*:145). Sasha breaks two social expectations (as other Rhys heroines do): that women should not drink strong drinks (she likes Pernod), and that they shouldn't drink alone. But she has been doing both a long time. She remembers, long ago, drinking absinthe with her husband Enno, becoming "quarrelsome" and then not sure if she had yelled at Enno and their companions or not. (*GMM*:122). She is much further along into addiction and its consequences than Rhys's previous protagonists: she has had the idea of "drinking myself to death" with "whisky, rum, gin, sherry, vermouth, wine . . ."(*GMM*:43). Her face is "gradually breaking up," though she wants to think of it as just a "tortured and tormented mask" (*GMM*:43). Of course, she is drinking as she imagines this. Rhys is once more extremely good at portraying the effect of alcohol on thought processes. When drinking, Sasha is unreasonable, self-pitying, aggressive and yet peculiarly aware of how she looks and acts to others. As she gets drunk on more Pernod, she thinks everyone knows she has come into the bar to get drunk. Women who do that "start crying silently. And then they go into the lavabo and then they come out – powdered, but with hollow eyes – and, head down, slink into the street" (*GMM*:107). Before and after seeing a film alone, she drinks Pernod, plans a bottle of Bordeaux for dinner, and then adds whisky. Very drunk, she looks out of the window and sees a man singing in the gutter and looking at her with two heads and two faces. The odd and interesting thing is that Sasha is both an entirely unreliable narrator (in reading the world through her drunken paranoia) and one whom the reader can trust to see herself with brutal clarity. Rhys so often makes alcohol a crucial factor in her novels: it is part violation of the normative codes of expectation for women, part a way to express the repressed inner core of her characters' emotional lives, liberated if distorted by the drug, and part story of the prevalence of drink in the cultural spaces Rhys wrote about, as well as in her own life.

This novel has hilarious performances of stories, in music-hall fashion, as Sasha tells jokes (especially around unmentionable subjects), does various (if often unnerving) pratfalls, and skewers people she does not like with apposite descriptions. The young Sasha can sound like Anna, in her mocking thought about Walter and the waiter, "Bowler-hat, majestic trousers, oh-my-God expression" (*GMM*:19). The older Sasha is not someone you would want to spend a lot of time with, even though she can be very, very funny in an edgy way. Very early in the text, she gives a hilarious but also bitterly ironical mock lecture on public toilets for women (claiming she has read a monograph on the subject; *GMM*:11). Public toilets for women are represented by Rhys as a series of culturally varied feminine underworlds, each reflecting its national location. In London, there is the British passion for orderly waiting in turn (even if the need for the toilet is desperate): "fifteen women in a queue, each clutching her penny" (*GMM*:11). At the time of the novel, public toilets cost a penny, which had to be put into the door of the stall to open it. In Florence, a pretty, "fantastically-dressed" girl (*GMM*:11) brings cakes for the old attendant, whom she hugs, kisses and feeds (a daughter?). In Paris, the city of love, the attendant sells drugs, "to heal a wounded heart" (*GMM*:11). René, the gigolo, sees toilets as demonstrating the vulgarity of the wealthy, "I've stayed in one so rich that when you pulled the lavatory-plug it played a tune" (*GMM*:169).

But, more specifically, the lavatory has long been a haunt of Sasha when she feels frail or hunted. She remembers one long ago, in her marriage to Enno, where she vomited and knew she was afraid she might be pregnant, because they had no money nor a settled place to live (*GMM*:121). The familiar *lavabo* at the Pig and Lily, where Sasha goes with the gigolo René the night she pays for their dinners and drinks, is upstairs, and "resplendent" (and thus a good bolt-hole for a nervous woman; *GMM*:155–6). She imagines the mirror there talks to her (she has had a few drinks). In another bar, after listening to René telling new stories about himself, she excuses herself "primly" and goes to another lavatory she knows well, this time downstairs. He comments that she is "always disappearing into the lavabo": she retorts, "What do you expect? . . . I'm getting old" (*GMM*:170). Later, in a mood to reject René, she thinks bitterly of the "comic papers in the lavatory" (*GMM*:185).

Sasha says the unromantic, unsexy English enjoy their "ration of rose-leaves," not because roses are about love, but because the leaves are "a gentle laxative" (*GMM*:157). Even a film that she watches has a character who manufactures "toilet articles": when a woman who has been pursuing him finally gives up the chase, she says, "Alors, bien, je te laisse à tes suppositoires"

(I leave you with your suppositories). Then Samuel, the ridiculous husband of the woman Sasha worked for as a writer in the South of France, forgets to buy his "suppositoires" (*GMM*:168). Though there is a tiny detail in *Voyage in the Dark* about the toilet, when Vincent rudely says he thinks Anna is going upstairs to curl her hair and she retorts that she is going to the lavatory, in *Good Morning, Midnight* it is a fundamental integrating element in the text.

Related to the *lavabo* theme is the bitter humour about another unmentionable topic: women's drawers (the 1930s term hardly ever associated now with sexual activity). Sasha remembers a lively woman friend of Enno's, Paulette, of whom she was a little jealous. One of her lovers was a Count, who wanted to marry her but his family disapproved. One day, after lunching with the Count's reluctant mother. Paulette was walking out of the restaurant when her drawers fell off. Sasha had a similar experience. A man wanted to have sex with her, asked her "can you resist it" (presumably his penis), and she answered "Yes, I can." So he buttoned up (his trousers), took her to the bus stop, and as they stood there waiting for the bus, "(m)y drawers fall off" (*GMM*:136). Sasha goes on: "I look down at them, step out of them neatly, pick them up, roll them into a little parcel, and put them into my handbag" (*GMM*:136). She gets on the bus presumably a little freer, not only of the unlovely would-be lover: drawers were not the most secure of garments and perhaps many women knew how to handle this sort of thing.

But now Sasha is getting older, needing better clothes, more comfortable shoes, taking longer to dress to face the world, but still damaging herself with strong drink. She has been sent to Paris because she is drinking so much she looks bad. A strange young man in a bar there refers to her there as "*la vieille*," the old lady (*GMM*:41). Sasha hopes dyeing her hair will make her appear less old. She is wittily philosophical about the process of removing one color before adding another: this makes "educated hair" (the removal of original identity to make way for what is approved by the system). She remembers an old lady she saw long ago calmly facing a mirror, trying to put hair ornaments on her bald head. An old woman asks Sasha for money, and "looks straight into my eyes with an ironical expression" (*GMM*:49), presumably seeing Sasha heading for the same fate. In an ironic revisioning of the happy idea of a young, sexual woman as an attractive "kitten" (such as Anna was called), Sasha remembers a doomed kitten she saw once in London, and then thinks her eyes and the kitten's are alike (*GMM*:56). She frets about the poor light in her rented room which prevents her seeing properly to put on her makeup. Even as a young woman, she was capable of being horrified at her reflection in a mirror (*GMM*:122); but she is willing to watch a girl putting on makeup at a window across the street until the girl notices and Sasha closes the window because she fears being watched herself (*GMM*:34). She is acutely aware of the pressure to conform. She spends three hours to choose a hat and an hour and a half every morning "trying to make myself look like everybody else" (*GMM*:106). She worries that her old fur coat marks her as a woman who once might have had some elegance and means, but now needs to buy sex or affection.

Geography is again important but this time refracted within Sasha's often befuddled mind. Early in the narrative, staying in Paris, Sasha is haunted by memories of years ago (1923 or 1924, or maybe 1926 or 1927), when she lived "round the corner, in the Rue Victor-Cousin" (*GMM*:12). Victor-Cousin is in the same neighborhood near the Jardin Luxembourg and the Sorbonne, which Rhys used so often for Paris locales key to her plots. Sasha drinks on Avenue de l'Observatoire, (where the Heidlers lived in *Quartet*), and sees a film on the Champs-Elysées (*GMM*:16).There she remembers going to work via the Rond-Point Métro station, walking along the Avenue Marigny: this is because the Champs-Elysées is close to the Avenue Marigny, both lying across the Seine from Montparnasse. The fake "olde English tavern" she enjoys (*GMM*:39), the Pig and Lily, is at the back of the Montparnasse station. She walks along the Boulevard St. Michel, close to her hotel, sits in the nearby Luxembourg Gardens, stands up a new acquaintance she is supposed to meet at the Dôme (so associated with Ford and part of the important geography of *Quartet*). She knows Montparnasse and the Latin Quarter are "side by side and oh, so different" (*GMM*:65), connoting her long acquaintance with these neighborhoods. Going to buy a hat, she thinks of a hat-shop she used to know years ago in the Rue Vavin, near the Luxembourg Gardens, but, not feeling confident, she wanders back streets. Later, lifted by a new hat and hairdo, she feels confident enough to go to the famous Place de l'Odéon, and to the Dôme (*GMM*:71). Her walks take in the Paris Panthéon, shrine to famous French male luminaries. René lives near the Gare d'Orsay, near Les Invalides, outside Sasha's favorite Paris locales.

She remembers being a terrible tour guide, standing in the middle of the Place de l'Opéra and failing to remember how to get to the Rue de la Paix: Rhys assumes her readers know that you only have to cross the Boulevard des Capucines, the main street the Place de L'Opéra faces, so it is very close. She later manages to take her clients to the nearby Place de la Madeleine. Going to meet Serge, who lives just off the Avenue d'Orléans, walking distance for her, she insists on a taxi. Delmar, her companion, has it drop them at the Place Denfert-Rochereau, the Métro station, near where Serge lives, because he doesn't know the name of the exact street, but she also notices he is very anxious about the meter, and offers to pay. She says she would have "dropped dead" if she took that walk (*GMM*:86). She is clearly not the easiest of friends.

Her memories sometimes conflate London and Paris. In a dream she is in London, trying to find an "Exhibition" (there was a famous World Exhibition in Paris in 1937, to which Sasha goes with René).[34] In a particularly chronologically layered moment, Sasha remembers a hotel in the Rue Lamartine where she stayed with Enno, her husband when she was young. Sasha once rented a room "just off the Gray's Inn Road," in the rather scruffy St. Pancras area of London. Both Sasha and her friend Serge once lived in Notting Hill Gate in London. A client to whom Sasha taught English during her marriage to Enno was on his way to Oxford. There are other places briefly mentioned, associated with the emotional ups and downs of Sasha's marriage to Enno, many years before: Delft, Amsterdam and Brussels (where Marya goes with Stephan also in *Quartet*). These sparse details deepen our sense of Sasha's past.

She is of dubious nationality, by her own account, when we meet her. But there are many references to nationality, race and ethnicity in this novel, as in previous Rhys fiction. Some are vague, as when characters are said to be "dark" (*GMM*:9), but many are specific. Sasha's Paris is very cosmopolitan (with English, German, Russian, Spanish, Dutch, Italian and Chinese people among the French). A "Turk," Alfred, befriends Sasha and Enno, though he is contradictory, both encouraging Sasha to give English lessons and then saying he would never let his wife work for another man (*GMM*:127). Rhys's text subtly emphasizes Sasha's awareness of outsiders, those who are different in their own sense of themselves or that of other people. She notices that Serge, the Russian painter, is Jewish: "He has that mocking look of the Jew, the look that can be so hateful, that can be so attractive, that can be so sad" (*GMM*:91). In other words, Serge has much the same repertoire of looks as does Sasha herself. Interestingly, he makes fake African masks ("straight from the Congo," he ironically describes them; *GMM*:91). African art was of course an important influence on European modernists, but in this case Serge is faking a product. He is aware of the Caribbean, for he likes Martinique music, and is aware of "Negro music" in Paris, and a Cuban club in Montmartre. He tells the story of a "mulatto" woman he met in London, from Martinique. She lived with an Englishman who did not appear to love her. She was very hurt by the insults of white English children. The gigolo, René, is of mysterious origin (he claims to be French-Canadian, Sasha thinks he is Spanish American and he ultimately admits to being Moroccan, therefore likely of mixed race). He is probably an illegal immigrant, who has come to France and to Paris without papers and has to use his wits to survive. He refuses to talk about Morocco. But he also proves that not all the marginalized stick together. He is highly dismissive of the Russians Sasha has met: "Russians in Paris! Everybody knows what they are – Jews and poor whites. The most boring people in the world. Terrible people" (*GMM*:163). A Hindu assistant in a bookstore insists Sasha buy a "very beautiful" book she does not want, on the white slave trade (*GMM*:132). Conflating race and gender, Sasha remarks that the desire in "some men to get you to swill as much as you can hold" whereas others "try to stop you" has to be "something racial," the result of some profound instinct (*GMM*:179).

As in previous novels, rooms are important here. Sasha finds that all hotel rooms seem the same. Sasha's room in Paris speaks to her: "Quite like old times . . . ", showing how she is recurrently trapped in anonymous spaces (*GMM*:9). She is aware that rooms cost more because of the way she appears: "One look at me and the prices go up" (*GMM*:34). This first one she secures is large, though faintly smelling of cheap hotel, and outside the street ends in a flight of steps, an *impasse*, suggesting that Sasha's life is also at an impasse. There are many kinds of rooms that are important in the novel. These include the "large white-and-gold room" (*GMM*:17) where Sasha remembers her work as a *vendeuse* of expensive clothes, "(t)he showrooms, the fitting rooms, the mannequins' room"(*GMM*:25), the cockroach-infested bathroom in a rooming house (*GMM*:33), the "nice room" someone is looking for to rent (*GMM*:34). Serge the painter has an "empty, cold" room (*GMM*:91); Sasha gets drunk in a bar which she calls a room (*GMM*:107); Sasha and Enno stay in the "*room at the Steens*'" (*GMM*:113); Sasha remembers a room she was glad to leave in London (*GMM*:113); Sasha and Enno stay in an Amsterdam room after their marriage (*GMM*:116). Then is the room in a Brussels hotel (*GMM*:118), the room in a hotel in the Rue Lamartine which has to be fumigated (*GMM*:125), and a hotel room near the Place de la Madeleine, with a lot of flies (*GMM*: 143).

As in Rhys's other novels, a room can be a shelter or a prison. A young dishwasher works in a foul-smelling, tiny room which is a "coffin" (*GMM*:105). Details of decoration in rooms are less evident than in previous fiction, but the same connection between emotional experience and wallpaper is clear in Sasha's memory of the room where she was happy with Enno, many years ago, which had "rose-patterned wallpaper" (*GMM*:116).

Houses also carry emotional baggage: one briefly sheltered Sasha's doomed baby (*GMM*:139). Houses can be dark and "sneering," and they can crush, As Sasha says, "Rooms, streets, streets, rooms . . ."

Though climate is not as key as in *Voyage in the Dark*, the weather impacts Sasha's mood. She marries Enno on a cold and wet day, and adds to the gloom by wearing grey and carrying lilies of the valley (white). Sasha is happy with Enno at first, "tuned up to top pitch" by love, which makes her notice the lovely colors in the sky or of lights on water (*GMM*:18). She is heavily pregnant in a hot summer. After the baby dies, Sasha sees the dark red, dirty carpet in their hotel room as a "dark wall in the hot sun", at the time of day when "everything stands still," a subtle but definite recollection of the Caribbean (*GMM*:140).

Popular culture is again interestingly detailed. Cinemas and films offer Sasha an escape from the real world but she worries about her "film-mind," because lurid fantasies torment her imagination. A French singer who performs at La Scala joins Enno, a former singer, in celebrating the marriage to Sasha, the Frenchman singing in English and Enno in French. Even Sasha sings, in English. A song sung by a man in the gutter is about being young and loving (*GMM*:185).

If *Voyage in the Dark* is about the cruel robbing of illusion from a childlike young woman, *Good Morning Midnight* is about a life sinking deeper and deeper into bitterness, self-destructiveness and the embrace of nothingness. Even a chance of affection is lost because of emotional damage. Sasha meets René on a night when her hair is newly done and she has a new hat and she treats herself to an expensive bar after dinner: he preys on solitary older women who seem to have the means to take care of their looks and therefore might be assumed to be willing to pay for a bit of sexual interest. But she has lost too many important emotional connections: her parents and family, Enno and her baby. Two tiny details give away that she once had the capacity for affection: she felt love for Enno when he looked anxious one day (*GMM*:129), and she called God "a devil" because of the loss of the baby (*GMM*:140). As the novel progresses, she loses the last chance of affection with René, who seems to care for her genuinely, and in a quasi-paternal protective way.

But, as in *Voyage in the Dark*, some women in *Good Morning, Midnight* are good at using men for what they need without being traumatized. The young Sasha admires Lise, the well-turned-out French woman, sentimental and self-dramatizing but a good friend. Paulette is more worrying, successful at using her body to extract money from men and close to Enno just as Sasha is hugely pregnant. Sasha is not good at getting what she wants. Enno soon complains she is boring, passive and lazy in love-making. He demands that Sasha serve him an orange: she obeys because he has come home with money. Enno forgets to cancel a client who was to come for an English lesson with Sasha, so she receives him sitting in bed as she is heavily pregnant. They read Oscar Wilde's play *Lady Windermere's Fan* together, a demure choice, but Sasha thinks he imagines she wants to seduce him.[35] This is never explained. Clearly Enno is careless, Sasha is heavily pregnant, yet sex hovers in the air between her and her student. Rhys's protagonists are not exactly innocents, but they are hopeless at manipulating a situation for their own gain.

Because Sasha is so inept at manipulating men for money, it is a huge irony that she begins a connection to René, who successfully gets women to pay him for sex. He boasts that he will do well in England, because it is not a woman's country: "Unhappy as a dog in Turkey or a woman in London." There, he says, it's a case of "(a)t least fifty per cent of the men homosexual and the others not liking it so much as all that. And the poor Englishwomen just gasping for it, oh boy!" (*GMM*:157). Sasha thinks he is a fool to imagine he can work London successfully, "he'll find out he will be up against racial, not sexual, characteristics. Love is a stern virtue in England," and a "matter of hygiene" (*GMM*:157). René is curious about her sexuality (perhaps because she resists him). He has tried boys "in Morocco" but "it was no use. I like women" (*GMM*:160). Sasha is bitterly ironical about that: "Then you ought to be worth your weight in gold" (in England, where by implication, there are few straight men; *GMM*:160). He asks her if she has ever been interested in women and she confesses that she once saw a girl she could have loved, "in a bordel" (*GMM*:160). But of course she never pursued it.

Part Four brilliantly intertwines threads established earlier in the novel, and culminates in a stream of consciousness (Rhys did something similar in *Voyage in the Dark*). This novel has again three important male characters, this time Enno, René, and the *commis*, a sinister man who stays in the room next to Sasha. Enno, who is important in Part Three, vanishes from Part Four, a sign that Sasha's hopeful youth has entirely gone. It is René and the *commis* who are important in this last section.

The *commis* appears one day in the corridor of the rooming house where Sasha is staying, in an "immaculately white" dressing gown, looking "like a priest . . . of some obscene, half-understood religion" (*GMM*:35). He has two dressing gowns, the white one and a blue one, and he is "like the ghost of the landing," almost like a zombi, a living-dead person. He is furious to find that René visits Sasha in her hotel room.

Rhys exploits the ironies of gender conventions when she has Sasha notice the gigolo's beautiful teeth (so reminiscent of evaluating people as chattels, and of Walter's appraisal of Anna in *Voyage in the Dark*). This is a sign that Sasha has put down heavy defensive protection against any feelings for the gigolo (the subtle reference to slavery indicates this well). The last interactions of Sasha and René are directed by Sasha's terror of intimacy. René can't quite work out why she is so afraid, and wonders if she might fear he will harm her (in fact when she thinks about that idea, she imagines she would agree to let him kill her). Her suppressed emotion is evident when her throat hurts and she cannot speak, and, when she does regain speech, she is violently angry, but expresses fear of people. Clearly there is some trauma underneath all this, which seems indicated by a sudden memory of "a misery of utter darkness." It takes her away from the present moment, so that, when she returns to consciousness of René, he is "looking sad." Perhaps because he wants to let her know he too has his scars from the past, he shows her a literal one, across his throat. Rhys captures the emotional chaos in Sasha by a series of small details: her feeling she has "screamed, shouted, cursed, cried" (*GMM*:174), her image of "the little grimacing devil in my head" (*GMM*:175), who wears a top hat reminiscent of the "little black boy" mentioned earlier. She also recalls a sadomasochistic fantasy of being forced to serve a man and other women, and of being ill-treated and betrayed by the man. This seems a version of the Mr. Howard material in Rhys's Black Exercise Book: here it is a very effective way of indicating how deep Sasha's sexual and emotional damage goes, so that even when René makes her feel young and happy it cannot last.

Of course she uses alcohol, and relies on a cynical humor, "I bet nobody's ever thought of that way of bridging the gap before" (*GMM*:178); she tells René to go to hell when he tries to stop her drinking. He keeps trying to find a way to get close to her, telling her she loves playing a comedy and he wants to see it, but the more he tries, the more she is afraid (that he will laugh at her, see her as old). Then he becomes irritable and frustrated and they struggle on the bed, with him trying to physically break into her, and trying to shock her with a story about how in Morocco you can have a woman easily by getting "four comrades to help you . . . They each take their turn" (*GMM*:182). Though Sasha feels she is dead, she does eventually feel something and cries, though everything hurts, as a numb limb might hurt coming back to life. But then she finally realizes the way to have him go: offer him money and reduce their relationship to a transaction.

Rhys writes Sasha's extreme drunkenness effectively so that it adds a terribly tragic dimension to the whole scene. She hears voices, one laughing, one crying, and knows that the laughing one isn't her. The gigolo has not taken her money, for which she is grateful. She remembers earlier experiences out of context: the "Russian's face" and talk about "Madame Venus," a flashback to a scene earlier in the novel (GMM:186). Rhys used such flashbacks in the stream of consciousness she gave Anna in *Voyage in the Dark*. She knows she believes in nothing. not Venus, Apollo or even Jesus.

All "that is left is an enormous machine made of white steel," with arms and eyes at the end of them, "stiff with mascara" (GMM:187). She is delusional, believing René can be reached by her will and made to come back, so she opens the door and takes off her clothes and gets into bed. We discover it is not René by the conceit of the dressing gown: Sasha asks which one it is. The *commis* looks down at her meanly. She looks into his eyes and thinks she will "despise a poor devil of a human being for the last time," and she puts her arms around him and pulls him down onto the bed, at the last moment of the novel, saying "Yes–yes–yes," which, as Howells points out, is an ironical echo of the words of Molly Bloom at the end of Joyce's *Ulysses*.[36] This is a deeply disturbing conclusion, but very powerful: a surrender to the end of love, a female wasteland.

Wide Sargasso Sea (1966)

In a 1959 letter, written whilst she was working on *Wide Sargasso Sea*, Rhys described her earlier novel, *Voyage in the Dark*, as expressing how "the West Indies started knocking at my heart." She added: "That (the knocking) has never stopped" (*L*:171). She felt she could only write "for love" about two places, Paris and Dominica.

Wide Sargasso Sea is a departure from Rhys's other full-length fiction. Firstly, the narrative is split between two first-person narrators, Antoinette, who opens and closes the novel, and her unnamed husband. Telling a good deal of this story in a man's consciousness had a kind of rehearsal in Sasha's appropriation of some aspects of sexual and emotional dysfunction associated conventionally with maleness. Then the story is highly intertextual with Charlotte Brontë's *Jane Eyre* (1847). Rhys's version is mostly a prequel, the story of the woman who is mad in the attic and Rochester when he was young, but in the last part Antoinette dreams of setting fire to the house, which joins Rhys's story to Brontë's.[37] Rhys revisioned *Jane Eyre*'s lurid description of the Creole wife, which reflected nineteenth-century British stereotypes about white Creoles, as well as the role of dreams and ghosts and the colour red in *Jane Eyre*. Brontë gave Rhys a wonderfully grand level of violence for her last protagonist: in Bronte's novel, the house is destroyed and Rochester is deeply scarred and loses his sight. The intertextuality with *Jane Eyre* also means Rhys can merely reference this violence without having to repeat it. In *Wide Sargasso Sea* the husband is not named, an effective retort by Rhys to the renaming or erasure of names performed by colonialists and planters: I refer to him here as "Rochester." The importance of self-naming and the misnaming of others as an aspect of dominance reverberate often in Rhys's fiction: after all, she renamed herself.

This story also gave Rhys a vehicle to explore her difficult outsider relationship with England. As for Brontë's novel, Rhys said in a letter (*L*:262) that she had "brooded over *Jane Eyre* for years." She was, she wrote, "Vexed at her portrait of the 'paper tiger' lunatic, the all wrong creole scenes, and above all by the real cruelty of Mr Rochester." She had reread *Jane Eyre* in 1957, when she felt she had nearly forgotten Creole. In 1958, she wrote: "It might be possible to unhitch the whole thing from Charlotte Brontë's novel, but I don't want to do that . . . I have got a plausible story and a plausible way of telling it" (*L*:153–4). She created a story full of Gothic romance, entirely different in tone and style from *Good Morning, Midnight. Wide Sargasso Sea* is a writing back to *Jane Eyre* done before such intertextuality became identified as a widespread postcolonial response to colonial literary canons. Rhys also deftly structures parallels that weave together the new story and the old, her novel and *Jane Eyre* (most evidently, a mad woman confined in a house she will destroy).

The challenge Rhys faced was how to find a voice for her madwoman that would still facilitate a coherent story. She managed this well. Antoinette's two narratives are both lucid, and connected by her memory of her three dreams (two remembered in the first narrative and the third the one that propels her to fire the house). We therefore assume this is one narrative, interrupted by "Rochester"'s story. Though the reader comprehends her, Antoinette is perceived as insane and violent in her English confinement, and she tells even the first of her narratives out of that place. Rhys's experience in Holloway prison, being evaluated as to her sanity, might have given her a way into imagining that condition.[38]

But Rhys wisely avoided writing a whole novel in the voice of the victim figure Antoinette. She chose instead to rest a great deal of the narrative on the unnamed husband, which meant making him human enough to carry a first-person narrative in the crucial center of the novel. It is extraordinary that Rhys created a complex portrait of the kind of severely emotionally damaged, upper-class Englishman who destroys a trusting young Caribbean woman (as she was damaged by her first important lover). She finally imagined the inner life in youth of the kind of man who in maturity had so caused havoc not only for her previous protagonists (Heidler, Mr. MacKenzie and Walter), but for herself (Lancelot Grey Hugh Smith). Her "Rochester" is quintessentially English, unlike the male lovers in *Good Morning, Midnight* (Enno, René, the *commis*) who are all European. Rhys is at pains to show that though her male protagonist and narrator is afraid of passionate love, he is, in his way, also a victim of England's implacable desire to raise upper-class men to make and keep money and take no emotional risks. There was something in such a man that had once attracted the young Rhys.

Wide Sargasso Sea is about devastating betrayal of sexual trust. The story has faint and ironic echoes of *Othello*: a white Englishman marries a beautiful woman in a British Caribbean colony. They are happy until he believes malevolent suggestions that she is insane and promiscuous, like her mother before her. We see her young and happy, but there are hints that she herself accepts a certain emotional instability in white Creole women, when she remarks that her friend Germaine is even-tempered, "unlike most Creole girls." Later, Antoinette's husband finds her eyes "disconcerting," "(l)ong, sad, dark, alien eyes" (*WSS*:67). These suggest she is quite different from any English girl, and they are also reminiscent of the eyes of other Rhys protagonists alienated from their surroundings. He wonders about her Creole nature: "Creole of pure English descent she may be, but they are not English or European either" (*WSS*:67). In Antoinette's early days, she is full of life, but wild, like the nature that surrounds her. Rhys allowed herself to be romantic about Antoinette: *Jane Eyre* is also romantic. It makes Rhys's novel both seductive and disappointing, in the way of sugar on the tongue.

But she was writing at the top of her game in terms of sheer ability to organize and execute a narrative: this time there are three uneven sections. The first section (61 pages) contains a enormous amount of scene-setting information: this is Antoinette's version (though we do not know her name for more than fifty pages). This is followed by her husband's long account (108 pages); Antoinette's last narrative, which takes us to her dream of setting the fire, is short (just over 13 pages long). For one section in the middle narrative the voice switches back to Antoinette, as she goes to visit Christophine, her surrogate mother, to ask advice about the failing marriage. As with Rhys's earlier fiction, the narrative is subdivided into smaller sections, mostly simply designated by a gap in the text, although sometimes by asterisks. Asterisks mark the shift back and forth between "Rochester" 's voice and Antoinette's voice in Part Two.

This novel is highly plotted, which makes it an appropriate prequel to the highly plotted *Jane Eyre*. Rhys uses flashbacks again but this time in a more coherent manner, so the story is more suspenseful. The story begins just after Emancipation, first in Jamaica (Coulibri Estate, the family seat of the Cosways). The female protagonist again loses the protection of family (her father dies, her mother remarries, their house is burned by angry ex-slaves, the mother goes mad and rejects her daughter). Once more an Englishman appears to offer love, but, as we understand from "Rochester" 's story, intense sexual passion both pleases and disquiets him. His angst about it lets the troublemaker Daniel poison his mind. Antoinette has lost one brother (Pierre) and Daniel's claim to be her half-brother is only used to enable him to harm her. Antoinette does have a surrogate mother in Christophine, but, since she was a slave and is a servant, she cannot protect very much, though she tries.

Once again Rhys uses chains of references that connect significantly. At Coulibri, during the fire, a menacing man likens Antoinette's family to centipedes. Then Christophine says Amélie "creep and crawl like centipede" (*WSS*:102). Centipedes in the Caribbean can grow large and have a poisonous sting, sharply painful for unallergic adults and potentially lethal for small babies: they are reputed to refuse to die unless they are cut up into pieces or entirely squashed.

The geography of this novel is broader. *Jane Eyre*'s plot references is set in Jamaica, so Rhys also sets the beginning of the story there but describes Coulibri as if it were her maternal family's estate of Geneva in Dominica. Jamaica is a thousand miles or so from Dominica (and the fictional Granbois), and "Rochester" speaks of the "interminable journey from Jamaica" (*WSS*:66). They are said to be in "one of the Windward Islands, at a small estate which had belonged to Antoinette's mother" (*WSS*:66). The geography of Jamaica and Dominica is, however, somewhat detailed. Spanish Town is actually on the outskirts of Kingston. Massacre is the actual village north of Roseau on the west coast of Dominica, from where Rhys and her family rode on horseback up a trail to her father's country estate of Bona Vista, which seems the model for Granbois. The story of Massacre is alluded to vaguely by Antoinette, who explains it was not slaves who were massacred there long ago. In fact, as Lennox Honychurch explains, in *The Dominica Story*, the "whole truth of the matter will now never be known"; it is likely that many Dominican Caribs were killed by an English expedition bent on securing settlements in the Eastern Caribbean.[39] Most of the landscape of the story is lushly romantic, a suitable backdrop for the story. Also the old Imperial Road, an aborted project in Dominica at the turn of the twentieth century, is obliquely mentioned when Baptiste comes to rescue "Rochester" from the forest. But when "Rochester" thinks he sees the remains of a road, Baptiste denies it (*WSS*:105).[40]

The national and racial identities of major characters also represent regional history and geography. Antoinette's mother and her beloved nurse, Christophine, are both from Martinique. Tia, Antoinette's childhood companion, is the daughter of Christophine's childhood friend. Antoinette's stepfather is English: his son, Richard, is schooled in Barbados, but afterwards in England. Though Mason has other West Indian properties, he is the new sort of planter, coming as slavery is ended, and trying to industrialize the plantation. He is not interested in knowing or adapting to local culture: his family eats English food. If the freed slaves are not keen to work for him, he plans to import labour from India (which of course happened extensively in Trinidad and Guyana but not in Jamaica). This threat or idea is expressed in front of the servants, shortly before the house is set alight. Antoinette's Aunt Cora is related to her father's family. She also married an Englishman, a common pattern for white Creoles, and she and Mason clash over his assumption that he truly knows the local situation.

Rhys tells the story cleverly, so that the reader must pay close attention to discover all the details, and it helps to know something of Caribbean history. Once again, money and sex are fatally connected. Sugar plantations were set up to make money, and Mason clearly has done so, though the novel is set just after Emancipation, when planters like him were furious at losing their control over slaves because it threatened their wealth. When he marries Annette, he acquires all her property through the prevailing law at the time. He tries to be an affectionate father to Antoinette, often visiting her during her eighteen months at the convent school and giving her presents. His idea of making her secure is to marry her off, using her mother's property and perhaps some of his money as a lure. "Rochester" is a younger son, whose elder brother will inherit everything through primogeniture, the English upper-class tradition that protects family property from division, so he is interested in marrying a girl he has never met in order to be secure. He will receive thirty thousand pounds, a fortune at the time of the novel. Antoinette is not involved until the wedding is imminent. After Mason dies, his son Richard takes over the arrangements: Antoinette resists. Much later in the novel, the reader learns that Aunt Cora quarreled with Richard over the absence of legal settlement to protect Antoinette financially, which Cora believed that his father would have made, so she gave her niece two rings to sell in an emergency. As he is taking Antoinette away from Granbois, "Rochester" remembers he had planned to give it back to her, but he will now sell it (*WSS*:173).

As in her earlier work, Rhys constructs dramatic confrontations between strongly drawn characters. Christophine establishes herself in the scene where she brings breakfast to the newlyweds Antoinette and her husband. Though she calls "Rochester" master, with conventional politeness, she calls her coffee "bull's blood" and the coffee which "the English madams drink," "yellow horse piss" (*WSS*:85). She tells him she will send the girl to clear up "the mess you make with the frangipani" (the wreath of flowers left on the bed the previous evening to mark the wedding night, following Eastern Caribbean custom). "Rochester" is a nervous young man at first, capable of being gentle, but after his marriage he gradually transforms into a controlling husband, greedy for the pleasure his wife can give him, but increasingly indifferent to her needs because he is so absorbed in his own.

As in previous novels, Rhys depicts sexual experience both discreetly (in terms of the physical act) and exactly, in terms of the way sex reflects the emotional quality of a relationship. Like *Voyage in the Dark*, this novel portrays the way a young woman is damaged by a self-centered Englishman, but Antoinette is far more passionate than Anna. Also sex is described through a male consciousness. After the wedding, consummation of the marriage is postponed by travel until they reach Granbois. "Rochester" appears somewhat straitlaced. On the wedding night, he overhears Antoinette preventing Christophine from putting scent in her hair, because she knows he does not like that. He first realizes her beauty during the highly staged ritual of their first night alone together, but she also appears to him to be a lonely child whom he rocks and to whom he sings. She tells a childhood memory of two huge rats sitting on her bedroom windowsill at Granbois, and how she was not afraid of them: they seem both a child's innocent imagination of animals and a sinister suggestion. Antoinette was also softened towards him before the wedding by his suggestion that she could hurt him. Rhys's protagonists tend to be attracted to male sensitivity or weakness.

After sex that night, he is affectionate, but, as their relationship continues, and Antoinette becomes "as eager for what's called loving as I was," she also becomes "more lost and drowned afterwards" (*WSS*:92). Displaying both the lust (abandonment of inhibitions) and eventual revulsion of an inhibited, colonially trained Englishman lost beyond his own cultural fortress, he becomes "savage with desire" after seeing Antoinette's dress discarded on the floor of her bedroom. After exhausting himself with her, he turns and sleeps, "still without a word or caress," despite which she wakes him with "soft light kisses" and a caring desire to cover him against a cold breeze (*WSS*:93). Rather like a younger version of Walter in *Voyage in the Dark* he finds her a child, but at times "obstinate" (*WSS*:94). Antoinette is devastated by his refusal to sleep with her after he receives Daniel's letter, so she visits Christophine to ask for a potion to make things right. But, ironically, he is feeling attracted to her again the night he drinks the potion and has a terrible nightmare and sickness. On that evening, Antoinette has lit nine candles to make an atmosphere, and he thinks she has never looked so "gay or so beautiful" (*WSS*:136). Afraid and horrified, he cannot feel sexual attraction to her after he recovers from the potion, but he slakes his sexual thirst and need for power and reassurance with Amélie (who has just fed him as if he were a child, so offering him a kind of maternal affection that makes him feel safe). But just before he takes a now mad Antoinette off to Jamaica, en route to England, he imagines that she has a thirst for anyone, but not for him, "(s)he'll moan and cry and give herself as no sane woman would – or could" (*WSS*:165).

Sex, violence and death are deeply connected. Antoinette provokes "Rochester" to tell her to die (literally), but he speaks of her "dying" many times in the sense of orgasm, "my way, not hers" (*WSS*:92). Death is both metaphorical and real. Antoinette explains to "Rochester" that there are always two deaths: the real one and the one people know about, and so her mother "died" when she was a child (*WSS*:128). Sexual passion can morph into violence quickly. Christophine notices the marks of violent sex on Antoinette's body and tells the story of a passionate couple she knew, and the wife's injury at the hands of her husband who loved her.

Lush flora add to the sexual intensity of the period of the early honeymoon but also intensify "Rochester"'s alienation from Antoinette later on. Flowers are sexual. These include the river-flowers, which only open at night, and an orchid which "Rochester" once took to Antoinette and later violently tramples on in his revulsion at her. There is a rich smell of cloves, cinnamon, roses and orange blossom in the air when "Rochester" and Antoinette reach the "honeymoon house," which he at that moment enjoys (*WSS*:73).

Once more alcohol is a key element. Antoinette and "Rochester" drink champagne on their wedding night (a sign of Dominica's proximity to the "Paris of the West Indies," St. Pierre, Martinique, from where Antoinette's dress for the evening came). But there is also wine on the night table when they retire, and they drink a glass each. This presumably helps both of these near strangers overcome their shyness with one another. Daniel drinks rum before and during his meeting with "Rochester": a direct question, however, seems to sober him up. Antoinette's husband drinks rum as he confronts Antoinette with what he has heard from Daniel. He empties the decanter and fetches another bottle and, whereas Antoinette had refused wine, "now she poured herself a drink," though she scarcely touches it (*WSS*:130). She remembers seeing her mother in confinement, being fed rum before one of her custodians kisses her on the lips. Antoinette feeds the love potion she has begged from Christophine to "Rochester" in wine. After he sleeps with Amélie, Antoinette's servant, Antoinette sends the butler for rum for herself. "Rochester" finds a chest full of bottles of "the rum that kills you in a hundred years, the brandy, the red and white wine smuggled, I suppose, from St. Pierre . . . " (*WSS*:144). He chooses to drink the rum. Both Antoinette and Rochester are fueled by strong drink when they have a fierce quarrel, Antoinette drinking defiantly through it. When "Rochester" snatches the bottle of rum (from which she has been drinking directly, without a glass), she bites him, and he drops the bottle, which smashes. Antoinette smashes another bottle and threatens him with a piece of broken glass (*WSS*:148). Even after all of this, "Rochester" looks for another bottle of rum and plans to have a strong drink before sleeping. But then Christophine confronts him. Rhys writes "Rochester"'s thoughts as an echo effect of Christophine's words, which cleverly suggests he is befuddled by the drink: " 'But all you want is to break her up'. / (*Not the way you mean, I thought*) / 'But she hold out eh? She hold out'. / (*Yes, she held out. A pity*)" (*WSS*:153). Christophine admits she has been trying to heal Antoinette with her own medicine, as well as with simple kind care, but when this seems to be failing, she gives her rum. The role of alcohol is similar in the lives of Rhys's young protagonists: it plays a role in first sexual experience, and becomes the drug of choice when heartbreak comes, only to be part of the reason for further rejection. In the final narrative, Antoinette steals "the drink without colour" on a regular basis from her guardian, the same Grace Poole as in Brontë's *Jane Eyre.* It is probably gin, this being nineteenth-century England. Though it is hard for her to drink down at first, showing she had been without alcohol a very long time, it clearly enables her dreams, her violence and her memories and her intentions.

Race is a key element in this story. But it is complexly portrayed and tangled with gender, class and national identities in Antoinette, and these designate her as different in complicated ways from those around her, just as Anna is different in *Voyage in the Dark.* Rhys visited Dominica with her second husband in 1936. Her account of the visit in "The Imperial Road" shows she found hostility to herself as a local white Creole, and was reminded strongly of the way race and racism informed her childhood. In the novel, the Englishman's gaze assigns racial characteristics according to how he feels. "Rochester" describes Antoinette as both "not English" (*WSS*:67) and as looking like "any pretty English girl" (*WSS*:71). Under the influence of rum, as things between them go awry, he thinks she looks like the servant Amélie (*WSS*:127). At first sight, he thought Amélie "a lovely little creature," but "malignant perhaps" and "half-caste" (*WSS*:65). After he sleeps with Amélie, he thinks her skin is darker and her lips "thicker" than he had thought (*WSS*:140). Daniel (who significantly says his real name is Esau) claims to be Antoinette's half-brother, by a slave woman her father impregnated and then set free. Daniel claims his half-brother Alexander will not speak against white people, because he has done so well from them. "Rochester" notices Daniel, the loser, has a "thin yellow face" (*WSS*:122). Amélie says some say yes, some say no, as to whether his father is the same as Antoinette's, but that he lives like a white person with one room just for sitting in, that he was once a preacher in Barbados, and that he has pictures of his parents in his house, and they are "coloured" (*WSS*:120). She says Alexander has made much money in Jamaica and married a fair-skinned woman: his son is Sandi, who looks like a white man. She says she heard Antoinette and Sandi "get married," but never believed it.

Antoinette understands race complexly. In many ways, racial issues and categories in *Wide Sargasso Sea* reverberate with those in *Voyage in the Dark.* Though white children benefit in her racially hierarchical culture, they do not feel in control if outside their fortress houses and other institutions that protect them. When Antoinette goes to school from Aunt Cora's house, she is intimidated by two children, one, a boy, who is an albino, and the other, a girl, who is "very black." They frighten her until she remembers to hate them. Also racial barriers are constantly breached. Her "cousin" Sandi protects her, though she has been warned off claiming him as kin because he is "coloured" (*WSS*:50). The nuns at her convent school are both white and "coloured," as are the girls. She wants to find love, even across forbidden boundaries. She hugs and kisses Christophine, whereas "Rochester" says he could not (*WSS*:91): "She trusted them and I did not" (*WSS*:89). Though she uses "they" like any colonial white to connote the specific cultural practices of black people – "They don't care about getting a dress dirty" (*WSS*:85) she wants to be thought an insider (this remark is made in explanation to the stranger "Rochester"). This is very much like Anna's comments to Hester in *Voyage in the Dark* about the "jumbie beads": Antoinette knows exactly how Christophine wraps her head-tie, "handkerchief," in the Martinique fashion. In making a close childhood friendship with Tia, she comes (as Anna was said to do by Hester) to be able to speak at will in what sounds to "Rochester" an imitation of a "negro's voice" (*WSS*:129). She tells "Rochester" how her mother worried she was growing up a "white nigger" and shaming her (*WSS*:132). But she is also called a "white cockroach" as a child (*WSS*:23) and a "white nigger" by Tia, who declares, "black nigger better than white nigger" (*WSS*:24). Amélie calls Antoinette "white cockroach," and Antoinette explains: "That's what they call all of us who were here before their own people in Africa sold them to the slave traders. And I've heard English women call us white niggers. So between you I often wonder who I am . . . " (*WSS*:102).

In a letter to her close friend and editor, Francis Wyndham, Rhys said that after "Rochester" betrays Antoinette with her maid, she has an affair with her friend Sandi, "then with others. All coloured or black, which was, in those days, a *terrible* thing for a white girl to do. Not to be forgiven" (*L*:263). But she made this barely perceptible in the novel itself, perhaps because interracial sex was a controversial topic in British publishing circles in the mid-twentieth century. When "Rochester" takes Antoinette back to Jamaica, before he takes her to England, Sandi manages to find her, both when "Rochester" is out and when she goes out driving (*WSS*:185). They kiss before parting for the last time, "the life and death kiss and you only know a long time afterwards what it is, the life and death kiss" (*WSS*:186). But, though intense, this love is almost entirely offstage.

This is the only Rhys novel saturated with the idea of an illicit and disturbing magic. That this novel's elderly, frail and addicted creator pulled it off seems like magic also. But to flirt with the supernatural risked exoticizing Caribbean culture. We learn from Rhys's letters that Diana Athill, Rhys's faithful editor, suggested that the young couple must be happy for a while at first (*L*:262). Rhys thought this was a good idea and added that wildly passionate love was described in Dominica, by "the black people", in terms of a spell: "she *magic* with him" (or vice versa; *L*:262), which becomes clear in the way "Rochester" first falls for Antoinette. Daniel also uses the idea of magic to plant anxieties in "Rochester"'s mind about his wife. He mentions that Mason "was bewitch" by Antoinette's mother.

Rhys explained that "Rochester" would remember everything from before drinking the potion offered him by his wife. In actual obeah, she said, it is reported that the god possesses the person who drinks a special potion and when they come to they remember very little. (*L*:262). Obeah, a syncretic survival and recreation of traditions by African slaves from different cultures, is not a religion (in the sense of having a community of believers), but a practice. Clients ask the practitioner to facilitate something, for good or evil, and the means used may be traditional healing methods, rituals or the promise of powerful effects (including the threat of death). The British saw it as a source of resistance to their authority, as well as superstition, and on both counts discouraged it even to the point of making it illegal and its practitioners subject to arrest.[41] The general strength of belief in powerful spiritual signs is reflected in the world of *Wide Sargasso Sea* when the rowdy crowd who threaten the family as the house burns begins to disperse after the family parrot dies in the flames, because it is so unlucky to kill a parrot.

Rhys made obeah a mainspring of the plot. When Annette marries Mr Mason a guest remarks that it is "evidently useful to keep a Martinique obeah woman on the premises" (*WSS*:30). Rhys is careful to make the child Antoinette *imagine* Christophine has the machinery of obeah (lurid details suitable for a child's ideas, "a dead man's dried hand, white chicken feathers, a cock with its throat cut"; *WSS*:31). But in response to Amélie's provocations, Christophine threatens to give her "bellyache like you never see bellyache. Perhaps you lie a long time with the bellyache I give you. Perhaps you don't get up again with the bellyache I give you" (*WSS*:102). "Rochester" learns from a book that untraceable poison is a tool of obeah (*WSS*:107), probably a white planter terror about the possibility of slave revenge. When Antoinette begs Christophine for help, Christophine denies that she has anything to do with obeah, "that tim-tim story," and in any case that is "not for *béké*," whites (*WSS*:112). Then Christophine does something that links her directly to African custom: she silently draws lines and circles in the earth with a stick and rubs them out (*WSS*:116). Antoinette notices a heap of chicken feathers in Christophine's bedroom, which reminds the reader of her suspicions of Christophine's obeah when she was a child. Daniel tells "Rochester" that Christophine is an obeah woman and had to leave Jamaica because she was put in jail for it (*WSS*:124). Rhys raises the foreboding, so that when "Rochester," feeling some empathy and attraction towards his wife, sees white powder on her bedroom floor and Antoinette says it is to deal with cockroaches, the reader knows better (*WSS*:136). "Rochester" gets confirmation from a magistrate in Jamaica with whom he stayed before the wedding that Christophine was found guilty of the practice there and jailed, as well as an offer of help from him to set the local police on her. This is the weapon he needs to separate Christophine from Antoinette.

The zombi image is also very prevalent in the novel.[42] A girl taunts Antoinette that her mother has "eyes like zombi and you have eyes like zombi too" (*WSS*:50). The zombi is the living dead of sinister reputation in association with Haitian vodoun, which Rhys also employs to great effect. After Daniel's intervention, Amélie says that "Rochester" "look like he see zombi" when he looks at Antoinette (*WSS*:100). Walking alone in the forest, "Rochester" comes across little bunches of flowers tied with grass, and laid under a tree in a plantation run wild (*WSS*:104), sees a child run away from him frightened, and feels he has to ask Baptiste, the butler who comes to find him, if there is a "ghost, a zombi there?" (*WSS*:106). The old book he found at Granbois defined a zombi as not only the living dead, but sometimes the spirit of a place, needing propitiation by offerings (he thinks of the flower bunches he saw; *WSS*:107). Christophine thinks Antoinette's intense grief over "Rochester" gives her the look of, a *soucriant*, and even a dead woman, something menacing and ghostly. After "Rochester" wakes feeling he has been buried alive (the zombi theme again), he finds a bitter residue in his wine glass from the night before. After this, his vengeance on the woman who made him love her beyond his sense of safety is to turn her into the living dead, in effect a zombi, resistant, with "(b)lank lovely eyes" (*WSS*:170). He thinks of her as a zombi as he takes her away: "they walk and talk and scream and try to kill (themselves or you) if you laugh back at them. Yes, they've got to be watched" (*WSS*:172).

Catholicism and obeah mingle and separate in Antoinette's culture. Both as a child and an adult, she notices symbols of Catholic faith such as religious pictures in Christophine's room. The major cultural influence on Antoinette as she grows up after the fire is the powerful Catholicism of her convent school, and there are many references to hell and devils in the novel. Antoinette is never more of a spoiled white girl than in hurling a curse at Christophine as a "damned black devil from Hell" (*WSS*:134), similar to Rhys's account in *Smile Please* of her childhood anger at her nurse. "Rochester" on some level knows he might be "bound for hell," which he prefers to "false heavens" (*WSS*:170). Myra, the servant who betrays Pierre when Coulibri is set on fire, thinks everyone goes to hell, unless saved by her particular religious sect (*WSS*:35). Antoinette calls the man who kisses her mother "black devil" (*WSS*:147).

Though this novel is in many ways an important departure from Rhys's previous work, there are still significant connections. Letters are crucially important, especially those from Daniel, who claims to be Antoinette's half-brother and who betrays her. Mirrors are also once again important. Antoinette's mother perhaps "had to hope every time she passed a looking glass" (*WSS*:18). When Tia throws a stone at Antoinette, Antoinette looks at Tia (who has tears on her face) "as if I saw myself. Like in a looking glass" (*WSS*:45). In the convent, though there is no looking glass, a new young nun from Ireland looks into a cask of water and smiles at herself. The bedroom in the "honeymoon house" has a large looking glass in it. As Antoinette tells the story of the rats, she says, "I could see myself in the looking-glass on the other side of the room" (*WSS*:82). During her happiness with "Rochester," she often smiles at herself in her looking glass (*WSS*:91). When "Rochester" overhears Antoinette and Amélie quarrelling, he sees them both via their reflection in the looking glass in Antoinette's bedroom (*WSS*:100). Antoinette talks about her mother's anxious staring into a looking glass (*WSS*:130). It is important that Antoinette has no looking glass in her room in "Rochester"'s English house. She remembers that, when her husband refused to call her by her right name (he calls her Bertha now), she saw "Antoinette drifting out of the window with her scents, her pretty clothes and her looking glass" (*WSS*:180). In her last dream, which predicts her torching of the house, Antoinette sees an image of herself as a ghost in a mirror (*WSS*:188–9).

Also dreams, whilst present in other Rhys novels, are structurally crucial in this one. Antoinette has a dream three times. The first is when she still feels safe at Coulibri, but the dream is terrifying: she is in a forest, pursued by a someone who hates her, unable to protect herself (*WSS*:27).The second time this dream has vague but definitely terrifying sexual implications, as Antoinette sees her beautiful long white dress soiled in the dirt as she follows a man who looks at her with a face 'black with hatred" (*WSS*:60). She tries to hold onto a tree to save herself, but the tree rejects her. To a nun, she says she "dreamed I was in Hell," and is told the dream is evil (*WSS*:60). The third dream brings together all of her life and propels her to set the fire and leap from the roof of the house. But the difference between reality and dream or fantasy is a consistent concern to the novel's major characters. For "Rochester," reality is England, and Granbois becomes a "nightmare" from which he hopes he can wake (*WSS*:119). For Antoinette, England is a fantasy, like a dream (*WSS*:103), and one of her friends who went there to live said it was a "cold dark dream sometimes," from which she wanted to wake up (*WSS*:80). When "Rochester" first finds his wife appealing, he still thinks "this is unreal and like a dream" (*WSS*:81). When he rejects Antoinette, she sleeps badly – "And I dream" (*WSS*:113).

Performance and popular culture are key details here as in other Rhys novels. The novel's title was, Rhys said in a letter (*L*:253), taken from "a Creole song . . . written by a cousin of mine." Amélie sings about the white cockroach (*WSS*:101). Literary references have subtle but important reverberations. "Rochester" finds and reads old books at Granbois, but he also calls up vague memories of poetry he was taught, something he now hates. Two quotations are suggestive of what is in "Rochester" 's mind. "Pity is like a naked new-born babe striding the blast" is from a speech by Macbeth, debating the likely outcome of killing the virtuous and venerable Duncan: a chilling suggestion of some guilt over his absolute lack of pity and vengeful attitude to Antoinette. "Rose elle a vécu" comes into his mind as he touches a rose in a jug and the petals fall: this is on the morning after the wedding night (*WSS*:86). This is a partial line from François de Malherbe's poem on mortality, "Consolation à Monsieur Du Périer (gentilhomme d'Aix-en-Provence) sur la mort de sa fille" (1598). Malherbe wrote this moving poem for a friend who had just lost his daughter. The beauty of the dead girl has a brief life, just like that of a rose. So when the rose petals fall, they signify that fearful brevity, and in this case are a premonition of the brevity of "Rochester" 's happiness with his new wife.

There are commonalities between Rhys's previous novels and this one, but each time she employs a strategy in a different text, she makes it new.

Antoinette is seen as a ghost by girls in her husband's house in England (*WSS*:182). Popular art, whilst less common here than in previous novels, is represented by "The Miller's Daughter" (*WSS*:36). The parrot says "Qui est là" ("Who is there?"; *WSS*:41), as Sasha did when surprised by René (*GMM*:177). Baptiste retreats behind a "service mask" when "Rochester" asks him questions in the forest (*WSS*:106): masks are important in earlier Rhys novels.

But *Wide Sargasso Sea* and *Voyage in the Dark* have the closest connections. Family losses in each heavily impact the protagonist and become a factor in her lack of protection against what happens to her later on. Rhys calls up plantation history in both novels through white male relatives of her protagonists who are casual about interracial sex (Cosway and Bo). Black servants in each novel have a close emotional tie to the central character (Francine and Christophine). The colour red signifies (this is also related of course to *Jane Eyre*), there is a house in the hills (Morgan's Rest and Granbois), and there is a strong sisterly connection between the white female protagonist and a black slave or poor girl (Maillotte Boyd and Tia).

After *Wide Sargasso Sea*, in the collections of stories published in Rhys's seventies and mid-eighties, she affirmed once more her ability to tell stories in highly innovative ways.

Tigers Are Better-Looking (1968)

This collection of stories appeared two years after Rhys's triumph with *Wide Sargasso Sea*. She was seventy-eight years old. All of these stories were previously published. The first half of the collection contains eight stories, six from the early sixties and two from 1966–7, and the second is a reprint of ten out of the original twenty-two in *The Left Bank* (1927). It was a master stroke by the publishers to bring those early stories back into availability just at the moment when Rhys was gaining many new readers.

The stories from the 1960s show that Rhys continued to experiment with point of view and narrative voice. She used ellipses in her longer stories as in her novels, for similar purposes, to indicate time passing, or to move the reader to a different perspective. It is interesting that the central characters in two stories are writers, given that Rhys rarely wrote about her own professional experience in her fiction.

The first three in the collection are told in the first person, the next three in the third, and then the last two, "A Solid House" and "The Sound of the River," use both in interesting ways. The first-person narrators are all female, but of different ages and cultural identities and locations: "Till September Petronella" (1960) is told by a young woman on a strained romantic weekend in England, "The Day They Burned the Books" (1960) by a young girl in the Caribbean, and "Let Them Call It Jazz" (1962) by a mature Caribbean woman, Selina, living in London. Selina speaks in a light Creole, a bold move by Rhys, who was an exile from Caribbean speech for so much of her adult life. The rest of the stories are told by third-person narrators, "Tigers are Better-Looking" (1962, set in London), "Outside the Machine" (1960, in an English hospital near Versailles), "The Lotus" (1967, London), "A Solid House" (1963, set during the Second World War in England) and "The Sound of the River" (1966, set somewhere in the remote English countryside). All of the stories represent complexities of human interaction, caused by misunderstandings, miscommunications and betrayals of love, fidelity, honesty, truthfulness or the protocols of civil society. Some characters are emotionally or psychologically unhinged. The great central theme here is the same as the novels, emotional damage from unhappy love.

In "Let Them Call It Jazz," Rhys worked from her own experience of noisily quarreling with a neighbor when drunk, and being taken to court and sent for psychiatric evaluation. Selina is confined in the women's prison in London, Holloway, the same place where Rhys was sent.[43] Much can be said about Rhys transposing that experience to a West Indian woman of color, because few West Indian women would have drunk alcohol at all in the time the story is set, let alone to excess as Selina does. She knows some "Martinique patois" (*CS*:168), so like Rhys she grew up in a multilingual Caribbean world. But oddly, given the high priority of education in the region and Selina's mother's financial contributions to her welfare, she did not go to school until she was twelve.

Rhys's fictional practice in her novels is reflected here in a number of ways. The light Creole voice in which the story is told is quite brilliantly executed. It was not Rhys's own, but is highly reminiscent of Christophine's voice in *Wide Sargasso Sea*: "She too cunning, and Satan don't lie worse" (*CS*:158). Like other Rhys protagonists, Selina notices looking glasses (two are in the furnished flat she rents from Mr. Sims) and did not have normal parental protection as she grew. Her father was a white man whom she scarcely remembers. Her mother was a "fair coloured woman, fairer than I am they say," and she left for Venezuela when Selina was "three-four." As with Antoinette in *Wide Sargasso Sea*, there was surrogate care: "It's my grandmother take care of me. She's quite dark" (*CS*:164).

Songs are important in other Rhys texts, but here they are central. Selina likes to sing and dance when she is drinking, including a song her grandmother taught her, "Don't trouble me now," about a man addressing a girl who abandoned him because he was poor but comes back because now he has money: "You without honour, you without shame" (*CS*:168). Selina thinks she sings better after drinking wine, but the story's crisis is brought on by her drunken singing. Her neighbors don't just object to that, but have the racist white British reaction to a London becoming more multiethnic, "At least the other tarts that crook installed here were *white* girls" (*CS*:167). This causes Selina to damage expensive property (a colored glass window).[44] The importance of song comes back when Selina is in prison, where she hears a song. After she is free, she whistles the song at a party, where a man "plays the tune, jazzing it up" (*CS*:175) and subsequently sends her five pounds to thank her. Selina first fears she let him take away "all I had" when he changed the song, but in the end she concludes "let them call it jazz" (*WSS*:175), because she still hears the song as it was in the prison. It is also important that Rhys makes Selina genuinely working class, going to England to find a future, with the money her absent mother sent and her grandmother saved for her, though her dress-making skills are in low demand.

The title story, "Tigers Are Better-Looking," has a journalist as the central character. He lives in London and writes for an Australian newspaper (giving him outsider cultural but insider racial status). The story opens with a letter (letters are so often significant in Rhys's work), in which he is addressed as "Mein Leib, Mein Cher, My Dear, Amigo" by his friend Hans, who accuses Mr. Severn of being among a crowd of "timid tigers waiting to spring the moment anyone is in trouble or hasn't any money" (*CS*:176). But, he goes on, "*tigers are better-looking, aren't they*" (*CS*:176). Hans stayed with Severn to heal a broken leg, but despises him, and has even drunk all the milk in the fridge before leaving. He gives one last taunt, "write a swell article today, you tame grey mare" (CS176). The weekly article Severn is working on is no good, because he can't get "the cadence of the sentence," otherwise known as "the swing's the thing" (*CS*:177).

"On the rebound" from Hans, looking for distraction in a pub, he picks up two women. One he knows (Maidie) and one he doesn't (Heather). He identifies Heather as self-possessed. Though she suggests a last drink for the evening in an overpriced club, she refuses more than a small amount of the whisky Severn buys.

Race is central to this story as it is to "Let Them Call It Jazz." Speaking of Heather, Severn uses the casual racist slang of mid-twentieth-century England for a person not completely white: "Disdainful, debonair and with a touch of the tarbrush too, or I'm much mistaken" (*CS*:181). He asks a drunken question of himself, why she isn't white (*CS*:181). The club has a diverse clientele and musicians, a mulatto saxophonist, and a woman Severn associates with Brixton (which became predominantly West Indian between the 1950s and 1960s), and imagines wants to work on a cruise ship going to South Africa (*CS*:181).[45] The woman in a "lovely dark brown couple" is highly scornful of Bloomsbury (where Severn lives), saying in a "high, sharp, clear and shattering" English accent, "I didn't come to London to go to the slums" (*CS*:181). Rhys clearly was depicting London becoming more multiethnic: when Maidie and Severn are arrested for drunken brawling, Maudie describes a frightened, well-dressed, "very dark girl," who was also being detained, and comments, "But it isn't the pretty ones who get on" (*CS*:186). When Severn returns home, he finds the "tormenting phrases" that have haunted him are gone (such as Hans's "tigers are better-looking"), and that he now has the "cadence of the sentence" (*CS*:188). This is a rare glimpse into Rhys's sense of the challenge of writing well.

"The Sound of the River" is haunting. It begins with third-person narrative: a couple is in bed, talking, and we enter in the middle of their conversation, just as the woman is expressing unfocused fear. It is a large fear, worse than the little fears she can recognize and name. On their walk earlier, she worried that the river was too silent, as if it were full. Now, lying in bed, she remembers her mother trying to teach her to deal with fear: "You're not my daughter if you're afraid of a horse" (*CS*:237). Her fear is persistent but vague. In the morning her husband is dead in bed. The doctor wants to know if she heard anything in the night, but she says she thought "it was a dream" (*CS*:240), and she admits she waited too long to go for help because of the sound of the river: it "got louder and closer and it was in the room with me." Rhys is very good at Gothic touches like this. This story was based on the circumstances of the death of her second husband Leslie. Angier commented on the extraordinary willingness of Rhys to write such a self-critical piece.[46]

In "The Day They Burned the Books" the narrator (who has clearly had to memorize Wordsworth's daffodil poem along with so many other colonial children) is a literary child who is friendly with Eddie, a boy whose hard-drinking English father, Mr Sawyer, is agent for a small steamship line running between the islands and South America.[47] He calls Eddie's mixed-race mother "the nigger" or the "gloomy half-caste" (*CS*:152). Mrs. Sawyer is reported to react calmly on the surface but with "soucriant's eyes" (*CS*:152), but she stays, because of her material comfort. Mr. Sawyer buys many books from England.

After Mr. Sawyer suddenly dies (did Mrs Sawyer fix that?), the two childen enjoy the room of books. But then Mrs. Sawyer takes a grim pleasure in stripping it: she makes a pile to be sold and a pile to be burnt. The first pile has major male English poets (Milton, Byron), to be sold, but a good edition of Christina Rossetti is to be burned. Mrs. Sawyer dislikes all writers but feels more negative about women writers: men "could be mercifully shot; women must be tortured" (*CS*:155). Commenting on the old accusation that fiction is lies, Eddie says his mother lies, but "can't make up a story to save her life" (*CS*:156). The children steal a book each, a damaged copy of Kipling's *Kim* for him, a book that turns out to be in French, *Fort Comme La Mort*, which "seemed dull," for her.[48]

"Till September Petronella," "Outside the Machine," "The Lotus" and "A Solid House" are all centered on women struggling to make their way in a difficult world. "Petronella," like *Quartet*, has four characters, two men and two women, who perform an elaborate emotional dance during a weekend together. The men are seriously engaged with the arts. Julian (Frankie's man) is music critic for a daily paper and Marston is a painter. Frankie is quite successful as a model and keen on opera. Petronella has a far less impressive background, as a former unsuccessful chorus girl who is entirely ignorant of opera. She is also far less genuinely keen on Marston than he is on her, and develops a futile attraction to Julian. The tensions between the four characters are finally disturbing enough that Petronella takes herself off alone to get back to London.

In "Outside the Machine," Inez is in an English clinic near Versailles. Machines are frequently referenced. It is important that this is an English environment where Inez feels some women enjoy setting machines onto others to crush them, or identify as parts of an efficient machine when at work. The machine represents the English class system. Inez worries that, because she is outside it, she might be picked up by "a pair of huge iron tongs" and put "on the rubbish heap" (*CS*:193). The day Inez is to leave, she feels weak, as if she has to wait until "they came with the tongs to throw her out" (*CS*:208). But at the last moment a French woman hands her a handkerchief with money inside, sensing that Inez doesn't have any money or anywhere to go to recuperate. Despite this act of kindness, the last lines of the story are reminiscent of Sasha's view of the inevitability of self-destruction in *Good Morning, Midnight*: "Because you can't die and come to life again for a few hundred francs. It takes more than that. It takes more, perhaps, than anybody is ever willing to give" (*CS*:209).

"The Lotus" begins dramatically with dialogue: " 'Garland says she's a tart' " (*CS*:210). The woman, Lotus Heath, is a writer, trying to finish a novel about "a girl who gets seduced" (*CS*:210). She drinks and smokes, is clumsily made up, grateful for any company, middle-aged, and generally considered highly eccentric by her neighbors. This is a story about the worst that can be thought about a woman writer. Lotus declares her cynical manifesto: "don't be gloomy . . . don't write about anything you know . . ." (*CS*:212). Such things upset the middle-class readership. She also declares she dislikes the novel: "Only to make some money, the novel is" (*CS*:213). She prefers poetry and then insists on reciting a new poem. The man who invited her, Ronald, thinks she is "damned comic . . . the funniest old relic" (*CS*:215); whereas Christine, his wife, rages about the slum they live in and "this creature, who stinks of whisky" (*CS*:215). As if determined to prove every wild accusation made about her, Lotus later runs up the street naked and is arrested. The middle-class enclave is intruded upon by police trying to interview every resident in the building and so normality needs to be restored, which is why Ronald finds his wife suddenly attractive because she can ignore what just happened (*CS*:220). Lotus, on the other hand, has been carried off on a stretcher, out of sight.

"A Solid House" begins during an German air raid during World War II. It is set outside London in an unspecified place: "the square outside was calm and indifferent, the trees cleaner than a London square" (*CS*:222). Angier thinks this story is based in Rhys's experience in Norwich, in 1941, recovering from some kind of breakdown.[49] Teresa, the central character, hides with the house's caretaker, Miss Spearman, in the cellar as bombers fly over. This stress isn't helping her keep calm. Her fragile emotional and mental state is clear in her seeing the day as "glittering, glaring" and "heartless . . . acid, like an unripe gooseberry," with a "cold yellow light" (*CS*:228); she sees a similar "hard, bright glitter" in Miss Spearman's face. In her tortured imagination she wonders what would happen "[i]f they were to laugh until their mouths met at the back and the tops of their heads fell off like some loathsome over-ripe fruit" (*CS*:230). She feels she really "died" at the time of her attempted suicide (*CS*:230). Normal people are supposed to be "exactly like everyone else" (*CS*:231; Sasha in *Good Morning, Midnight* felt this pressure too). Practical, frugal and unimaginative Miss Spearman loves the occult and has a circle of people who like to play with it. But Teresa finds horrors in even very peaceful environments, like the ornate sitting room full of pictures, books, ornaments and furniture in quietly pretentious bad taste. Rhys captures a voice on the very edge of madness: "Heaven will never, never lack the sense of superiority nor the disciplined reaction nor the proper way to snub nor the heart like a rock nor the wrist surprisingly thick. Nor the flower of the flock to be sacrificed" (*CS*:234). By the end of the story, Teresa has found a way to sleep so that the "crash in her head became fainter" (*CS*:235).

Sleep It Off Lady (1976)

This collection of sixteen stories contains only three previously published stories, and appeared just three years before Rhys's death in 1979 at the age of eighty-nine. "The Chevalier of the Place Blanche" is Rhys's "much-adapted translation" of a story by her first husband Jean Lenglet (written under his pen name of Edouard de Nève), and represents their close collaboration as writers.[50] Diana Athill rightly comments that "Who Knows What's Up in the Attic" and "Sleep It Off Lady" are "extraordinary" portraits of the experience of old age, an unusual literary subject (*CS*:ix).

The order of the stories roughly follows the settings of Rhys's own life chronologically (the Caribbean, London, Paris, and London again, during the War). The final story is even beyond old age, a haunting imagining of returning home to the Caribbean after death, as a ghost. Rhys is always experimenting with narrative voice, whether in long or short fiction. Nine stories are told in the third person and six in first-person narrative. "Fishy Waters" is told through most effectively juxtaposed letters to a Dominican newspaper, followed by a summary of a lead article in the same paper and finally a third-person, all-seeing narrator voice to conclude. Rhys sometimes uses a distancing third-person voice for something so intensely remembered in her own life that it cannot be told more intimately.

"Good-bye Marcus, Good-bye Rose" is an extraordinary fictionalized account of the "Mr. Howard" story contained in Rhys's "Black Exercise Book" (see page 4 above). The third-person narrative makes the story even more sinister as it represents the sexual and emotional abuse impassively. Captain Cardew is an elderly war hero, visiting the West Indies with his wife. He takes the twelve-year-old Phoebe to the Botanical Gardens, touches her breast (inside her blouse), and on subsequent walks, rather than touching her, spins stories of sexual love that involve "(v)iolence, even cruelty" (*CS*:287). Both his wife and Phoebe's mother seem to notice something is going on, but direct their suspicions to Phoebe rather than protecting her. The wife takes Cardew away prematurely. The piece ends with Phoebe thinking that her "childish" desires to find a good husband and have children she would call Marcus and Rose are now irrelevant: she has lost a key piece of her innocence and ability to trust, and, somewhere deep down, blames herself for what happened, as victims of abuse so often do.

The first-person narratives that are most clearly autobiographical in tone are on the whole disappointingly slight (perhaps too protected). "On Not Shooting Sitting Birds" begins: "There is no control over memory" (*CS*:328):

the point of the story is the connection of memory to story-telling. This narrator has some of the mischievous quality of Rhys's young protagonists (she goes out to buy a silk chemise and drawers before having dinner with a man she likes, more than hinting she expects him to see them). She remembers being lost in the Dominican forest as a child and that she came to England thinking she knew all about English people from the novels she read, details that directly connect to Rhys's own life. In "Night Out 1925" Suzy has the same name as the central character in Rhys's unpublished first novel, "Triple Sec," and has read Francis Carco's books about seedy life, as Rhys did. Suzy goes with a man to a Parisian bar where scantily dressed young women try to earn large tips by simulating sex or pretending sexual attraction to clients. It is odd to be a woman in a place designed to appeal to men: the girl Suzy picks feels obliged to do something to respond and kisses Suzy's knee and her lip. Since Suzy gives the girls at their table far more of a tip than her companion instructed (and out of his wallet), he is annoyed. He resents too much common cause between women.

"The Bishop's Feast" is a fragment of memoir, originally part of the "Imperial Road" manuscript. "Heat" is a short piece on the eruption of Mt. Pelée in Martinique (1902) and the famous Dominican Boiling Lake. Both are of most interest to scholars researching the contexts of Rhys's life and work. "Overture and Beginners Please" and "After the Deluge" are about the life of a chorus girl, part of Rhys's preparation for her autobiography, because they include details directly from Rhys's own experience (leaving the West Indies and attending the Perse School in Cambridge in "Overture," being in a company touring around Britain in "Deluge"). Daisy in "After the Deluge" is a memorable character, an accomplished and quite devastating gossip, as well as an absolute narcissist who crashes to the floor, taking down a small table, when she hears the narrator angrily deny gossiping about her (*CS*:312). "Overture" is less successful as a story and reads more as a piece of rather stiff memoir.

"Rapunzel, Rapunzel" is a sinister little first-person narrative about a stay in a convalescent home, where an elderly patient brushes her long, silvery-white hair. One day, this patient asks for the ends of her hair to be trimmed but the male barber simply chops it all off: afterwards, the woman loses the will to live and soon dies. This nasty little fairy tale works because the first-person voice is only observing, giving nothing away: like all fairy tales, the cautionary aspect of this one is very clear. "Who Knows What's Up in the Attic" is third-person narration, about an old lady living alone, receiving a man selling clothes door to door and a visitor from Holland who is anxious about her and takes her out: this is a piece of Rhys's actual life in old age, but she presumably needed the distancing narrative voice to get her writerly balance.

Other third-person narratives are of variable quality. "Kikimora" is too short to be an effective story, but it is another example of Rhys's clever portrayals of the effect of alcohol on women with suppressed anger towards wealthy and powerful older men. "The Insect World" is set in wartime. A young woman feels anxious about insects (both in a novel she is reading about the tropics and in her own memories), but in reality her fears are more about getting older.

"Sleep It Off Lady" is, however, an extremely effective story, where the third-person narration correlates to the indifference of the world to elderly Miss Verney. She lives alone in a cottage. She sees a huge rat in the shed in her yard, but since she drinks quite a bit (the neighbors know because they carry her heavy dustbin, full of bottles, to the gate each week), the man she asks for help thinks she is seeing things: "Are you sure it wasn't a pink rat?" (*CS*:379). Her cleaning woman, Mrs. Randolph, complains she has had to pick up the contents of the dustbin, which she thinks was upset by a stray dog. Miss Verney is sure it was the rat. She frantically cleans her house, and eats less, so there is less garbage. She is diagnosed with heart problems and told not to pick up weights. But one day, feeling stronger and happier than usual, she discovers the dustbin has been forgotten at the gate and she first carries it in and then the heavy stones which are to protect its lid from removal. As she lifts her pail to empty it into the dustbin, she passes out, and comes to with the food she was throwing out all over her, eggshells and stale bread. She finds she cannot move. A twelve-year-old child, who lives across the street, comes when called but, in response to Miss Verney's request for help, says everyone knows she drinks, so "Sleep it off, lady" (*CS*:385). In the morning, she is found unconscious by the postman, and dies soon afterwards, "of shock and cold" (*CS*:386).

There are two striking and related stories about Dominica, "Pioneers, Oh, Pioneers" and "Fishy Waters." "Pioneers, Oh, Pioneers" is told complexly, beginning with two young sisters, Rosalie and Irene, who are clearly in Roseau, Dominica in 1899 (the same Market Street as is mentioned at the opening of *Voyage in the Dark*). They comment on the eccentrics in their small community, like Mrs. Menzies, Jimmy Longa, and Mr. Ramage. Rosalie is said to have fallen in love with Ramage when she was seven, two years ago. Rhys would have been nine in 1899, the same age as Rosalie, and, since Rhys's father was Welsh, the detail of the picture in Rhys's childhood home of the famous Welsh town of Bettws-y-Coed seems to be right out of direct memory. After an ellipsis, typical of Rhys's modernist narrative strategies, the narrative point of view switches to the girl's doctor father, Dr. Cox, and then to a third-person account of Ramage's arrival in the island, his purchase of a small estate buried in the forest, his marriage to a "coloured girl," and his growing strangeness, which includes wandering the forest naked but for his tools or lying naked in his hammock. The local paper reports not only the scheme for settling the "Imperial Road," the project of Hesketh Bell, the Administrator, but the oddity of Ramage. Local people begin to throw stones at his house, especially as his wife has disappeared and there are rumors that he might have done away with her. One night he appears dressed in white on his verandah to confront the stone-throwers, looking "like a zombi" (*CS*:283), and shortly afterwards is found mysteriously dead in his house, with all the windows and doors open. His wife turns up for the funeral, having been brought back from a visit to relatives in Guadaloupe (for which she departed suspiciously, in a fishing boat from the opposite side of the island). The story ends with Rosalie writing a love letter to the dead Ramage and her mother throwing it away whilst her daughter sleeps.

"Fishy Waters" is even more complex in structure. It concerns Jimmy Longa, who was mentioned in "Pioneers Oh Pioneers," and tells the story of the investigation of his alleged assault on a little black girl, told most effectively via letters to the local newspaper and a long and detailed account of Longa's trial, and the story ends with a third-person narrative about the fate of the little girl. It is one of Rhys's most deceptive stories, which rewards patient, close reading. The first letter is signed "Disgusted," in the manner of newspaper correspondents across the British colonial world dealing with touchy subjects and protecting their identity. This first letter describes Longa as a white British socialist, who lost a room in a boarding house for that reason, and was then criticized for living in a "predominantly negro quarter" (*CS*:298). Then the incident with the child occurs. Some people think he is a scapegoat (victimized by the white plantocracy). Presumably this letter is written by someone from the mixed-race elite. In late nineteenth-century Dominica this was characterized by a feisty involvement with the press and a continuous battle with the colonial English presence in the island. The next letter is signed Ian J. McDonald, who is presumably of the white elite, because this man attacks the first writer for trying to stir up racial hatred and argues that slavery originated with African chiefs. The third letter, signed by a local merchant called Kelly (presumably of color), attacks McDonald for omitting the greed of white merchants and planters. Then an anonymous "defender of justice" points out that the case ought not to be discussed before trial and the Editor of the paper shuts down the exchange. Another letter is from "Maggie," the wife of Matt Penrice, who discovered Longa with the little girl, but who is himself acting strangely, so they have plans to move from the town to a decaying small estate in the country.

The newspaper account of the trial follows. Matt Penrice describes how he came across Longa, standing over a naked, unconscious little girl who was lying on a plank laid on trestles, with a saw in his hand that was touching the little girl's waist. Penrice said he saw the child's body was covered in bruises. But there is something fishy about Penrice's story of his activities that day, not only his route to the Club and the time he left (unusually early for his routine), but the fact that he did not take the injured child to the hospital but to a former servant of his, Madame Joseph, to whom he had given a house when she left his service. Thus the little girl is kept away from talking to anyone but the doctor and Joseph, and the claim is made by the doctor that she refused to talk about her experience. Longa admits to drinking heavily and to wanting to scare the child as she was one of a group of children who had been tormenting him. He says he didn't think it odd that she was naked, making a racist inference, "they very often are, especially on hot days" (*CS*:307). The magistrate finds there is no direct evidence that Longa attacked the child, but it is distinctly odd that he didn't notice her injuries if he did not inflict them. Longa is to leave the island at the government's expense and return to England. But then the story moves to the Penrices', and the plan to send the child to be adopted by a friend of Madame Joseph in St. Lucia. It is clear that it was Penrice who beat the child. He plans to leave the island, but the story's final touch is that his wife feels she does not know him any more. He is a lost man.

The Collected Short Stories (1987)

Diana Athill, one of Rhys's devoted editors, put this collection together after Rhys died. It reprints all twenty-two stories from *The Left Bank*, as well as the eight stories in the first section of *Tigers Are Better-Looking*, and all of *Sleep It Off Lady*. In addition, Athill included five other stories, two published in 1969, "I Spy a Stranger" and "Temps Perdi," and two published in *Vogue* in Rhys's old age, "Kismet" and "Invitation to the Dance." There is also "The Whistling Bird," published here for the first time. Athill says that the last stories, from Rhys's time of failing energies, make her "feel sad" (*CS*:ix). They are less impressive than earlier ones but still valuable. "Kismet" is a fragment about chorus-girl life. "The Whistling Bird" is another account of the trip to the West Indies with Leslie in 1936, this time about a cousin called Liliane who was living in St. Lucia, a writer of songs, and perhaps the one who helped Rhys find the title for *Wide Sargasso Sea.*[51]

The description of a Creole woman walking into the narrator's hotel bedroom with a tea tray, wearing a bright-colored "high-waisted dress, a turban, and heavy gold earrings" (*CS*:397), is highly reminiscent of the description of Christophine in *Wide Sargasso Sea* when she brings in the morning coffee to Antoinette and her husband. "Invitation to the Dance" is again a memoir, about a childhood game and song called "Looby Li," which is vaguely suggestive and shocks adults into forbidding their children to play it.

The earlier stories, "I Spy a Stranger" and "Temps Perdi," are powerful. Laura in "I Spy a Stranger" is a strange woman trying to survive in a hostile rural community in England during the war. The attitudes of Mrs. Trant and Mrs. Hudson, who dominate this community, are reflected in the tone of the narrator who is conventional and rather formal. But this voice is interrupted by excerpts from Laura's writing in an exercise book (which is something Rhys did a great deal). Trant and Hudson discuss it: they've possessed it since Laura was sent off by taxi to a depressing "ugly house with small windows, those on the top two barred" (*CS*:255), an echo of the fate of Antoinette at the end of *Wide Sargasso Sea.* Angier comments that Laura's instincts are too literary for someone not a writer (one of the things that enrages Laura is a man kicking his dog which is called Emily Brontë).[52]

"Temps Perdi" is divided into three sections. The second and third are both numbered and titled, and deal respectively with memories from the protagonist's Caribbean childhood as well as her young adulthood in Vienna. Rhys of course had both these experiences. The first section begins in present time, during the Second World War in England, and then goes back in time. In Section 3, "Carib Quarter," the title of the story is explained as a Creole term for "wasted time".

The Caribs of Dominica live in a particular area of the island and are descendants of the people who occupied the Caribbean before Europeans came.[53] The protagonist remembers a visit to the Carib Quarter, which seems to be a memory of Rhys's visit to Dominica in the 1930s, with her second husband Leslie. The narrative has the tone of heightened personal recollection, or creative non-fiction: "The day we went to the Carib Quarter the wind was blowing luminous heavy clouds across the sky" (*CS*:270). It is the narrator's statement at the end of the second section that she will become "a savage person – a real Carib" (*CS*:267) that provides a link to the third section. This story was a remarkable step forward for Rhys into finding a voice for personal recollection – or, as we would say now, creative non-fiction, neither strictly autobiography nor fiction, but something in between.

Malcolm and Malcolm argue for more recognition of her considerable skill with the story as a genre, though they consider the content of her stories has a remarkable similarity over the fifty years or so of her writing career and A. C. Morrell sees Rhys's characters as "a society of types."[54] But her stories, like her fiction, do evolve, as she tries different modes of narration, and develops several types, such as the story as personal testimony, or the ghost story, like the haunting fragment, "I Used to Live Here Once," or the longer, more complex story that is on the way to a novella.

Smile Please (1979)

This unfinished autobiography was edited by Diana Athill and published in the year of Rhys's death. Rhys was nervous about other people writing her biography, perhaps because she had lived a life that was easy to misrepresent, in terms of bourgeois values, and she had a daughter to protect. But an autobiography was not easy to finish in her last years: she had already used up much of her life for fictional material and let what she did not need fall away in memory.

She did, however, complete a series of short pieces that give impressions of her childhood and adolescence, up to the time she left Dominica for London. The second section is preceded by a note from Athill to the effect that this was "not considered by Jean Rhys to be finished work" (*SP*:77). It is of course highly valuable to those wishing to understand this complex and enigmatic woman.

The intervention of David Plante as aid to the final stages of Rhys's work on *Smile Please* is troubling because he wrote an appallingly opportunistic betrayal of her trust.[55] Though the finished pieces end early in Rhys's life (her departure for London as a teenager), Athill's inclusion of work Rhys did not approve for release takes the story on to her marriage to Lenglet. There is also an extraordinary piece called "From a Diary: At the Ropemaker's Arms," and the book ends with two very short pieces, one about her life in Devon in her old age, "The Cottage," and the other, "My Day," first published in *Vogue*, about the same topic.

Angier dates "The Ropemakers's Arms" to 1952, and considers that without it "she could not have written *Wide Sargasso Sea*."[56] Angier argues that in this brutal and dramatic self-evaluation, Rhys puts herself on trial. The piece is written in gripping dialogue:

> PROSECUTION: *I suppose you will admit that the things that matter are difficult to tell?*
> Yes.
> *Impossible perhaps?*
> Perhaps, some of them.
> DEFENCE: *It is untrue that you are cold and withdrawn?*
> It is not true.
> DEFENCE: *Did you make great efforts to, shall we say, establish contacts with other people? I mean friendships, love affairs, so on?*
> Yes. Not friendships very much.
> *Did you succeed?*
> Sometimes. For a time.
> *It didn't last?*
> No.
> *Whose fault was that?*
> Mine, I suppose. (*SP*:132)

Rhys's skill in taking the chaos of inner life and dramatizing it very effectively is clearly demonstrated here.

Rhys's texts, whether short or long, are economical and layered, as poetry is, and able to accomplish a great deal in a short space. They are most satisfying to readers who enjoy discovering the language games she plays, because the political and cultural concerns that inform her work are accessed as much or more through her style as through what stories she tells.

Chapter 4

Reception

1927–1965

Ford Madox Ford's important "Preface" to *The Left Bank* confirmed Rhys's place at the modernist table. Subsequent early criticism demonstrates that his sense of her as a stylist was recognized by reviewers on both sides of the Atlantic.[1] Her work was seriously reviewed in important literary and cultural magazines and serious newspapers such as the *New Statesman, Spectator, Nation and Atheneum* and *Times Literary Supplement* in Britain and *New Republic* and the *New York Times Book Review* in the USA. She was compared to Katherine Mansfield.[2] Her first stories appealed to those who delighted in exploring literary techniques, even though her subject matter was already a problem for some readers.[3] Some reviewers, such as D. B. Wyndham–Lewis, saw her stories as "purely French," following Ford's comments in his preface on how much she had been influenced by young French writers in Paris, though the French connection did not please all reviewers.[4]

Rhys published steadily between 1927 and 1939, so that critics were able to watch her development over a fairly short period of time. *Quartet* received very positive reviews for its economical style and the powerful use to which Rhys put it for the development of character.[5] The bleakness of *After Leaving Mr. Mackenzie* was noticed by reviewers who nonetheless felt Rhys's style was outstanding.[6] The writer Rebecca West found the novel "superb."[7] In 1931, a review in the *Saturday Review of Literature* remarked on the relation of Rhys's style to poetry.[8] In 1935, an American review of *Voyage in the Dark* compared Rhys's style to Imagist poetry: "Put into words the thing itself . . . Out of that will come new, original beauty . . ."[9] The leading cultural and literary critic Cyril Connolly, thirteen years Rhys's junior, listed *Voyage in the Dark* among a few books he recommended to readers.[10] As with the earlier novels, *Good Morning, Midnight* once again drew high praise from reviewers for its style, but a good deal of complaint over its subject matter. A review of it in the *Times Literary Supplement* had a strong feeling of revulsion towards Sasha, the protagonist, even whilst admiring much about the novel.[11] Another review of it, in the *Spectator*, criticized Rhys's dependency "on dots," and much else about the style.[12]

In the same year, 1939, Jean Lenglet wrote the first overview of her fiction under his pen name of Edouard de Nève, by which he intended to introduce her to French readers to whom she was unknown.[13] He described her as outside all literary groups, working alone, a modernist with a brutally honest reading of the world of those outside society's norms. In 1946, John Hampson praised Rhys's clarity of style, whilst noting that she wrote about prostitutes with intelligence who usually drink too much.[14] In 1949, Alec Waugh connected her homeland Dominica (for him a place for those who could not fit in anywhere else) with Rhys's outcast characters.[15] These two strains of criticism, locating her in Europe or locating her in the Caribbean, both with some concern as to where she could belong, framed her work from early on.

A writer doing something different and doing it well needs an insightful critic to guide his or her new readers. Rhys was to have highly gifted and influential critics introduce her work later on, but in 1939, when *Good Morning, Midnight* appeared, she was little known. She was never a member of any literary coterie, and did not promote her own work. So she was very fortunate to have a champion in the sensitive and influential Francis Wyndham, who wrote an important essay on her in 1950, before he had been able even to read most of her work. He was perceptive enough to see *Good Morning, Midnight* as her best work (this was of course before *Wide Sargasso Sea* appeared, which tended to obscure the achievement of *Good Morning, Midnight* for critics). He wrote about her work several times. In 1956 he thought she was dead, and her work too little known. In 1963, he again emphasized that she deserved to be far better appreciated. Then, in 1964, Wyndham wrote an introduction for the publication of a part of *Wide Sargasso Sea* and said, rightly, that the Rhys of the pre-1960s had been ahead of her time.[16]

That she was, in her life and in the details of the style of her work, pretty much of a loner means that even some feminist literary history of the 1980s, seeking to provide a sense of female modernists, did not include her. She is not mentioned in *Writing for Their Lives: The Modernist Women, 1910–1940*. The authors, Hanscombe and Smyers, argue that "(m)odernism, for its women, was not just a question of style; it was a way of life," and that, because the radicalism of early twentieth-century women writers was a "simultaneous breaking with both literary and social conventions," this led to the making of a network.[17] But in Rhys's case the most radical aspect of her life was in her work, and she didn't join networks. Another aspect of her marginalization was that she wrote in English but preferred association with France, yet despite her inclusion in Shari Benstock's *Women of the Left Bank*,[18] as if she could be seen as contributing to modernism in Paris, her work did not begin to appear in French until the early 1970's.

But, as Angier points out, if Rhys had been in France or Russia, she might not have found early resistance to her work: Anglo-Saxon readers were less prepared to face "the realities of sex and money than the French."[19] Rhys unflinchingly wrote about self-destructive women whose fates were a combination of their own weaknesses and those of the men they encountered, which did not endear her to readers who expected a moral compass to be provided by contemporary literature, especially if written by a woman. F. R. Leavis (1895–78), the enormously influential moralist English literary critic, was beginning his career as Rhys began to publish but, despite his championship of emerging male modernists contemporary with her (such as Eliot, Pound and D. H. Lawrence), he did not notice her at all. Thomas Staley gives an account of the emphasis on the "moral, social and realistic" content of art as key for English writers in the 1930s,[20] something which Rhys of course ignored.

1966 and after

The mid-sixties in Europe and America was the time of the Civil Rights struggle in the USA, the emergence of the feminist movement, student protests at the state of culture and politics and an emerging consciousness of the postcolonial world. Social prohibitions against drugs, cigarettes, alcohol, abortion and promiscuity relaxed considerably in this countercultural moment. This meant that what had shocked or repelled earlier critics in Rhys works not only did not pose a problem to many later ones, but actually made Rhys seem as current as if she had been a young writer starting out. In addition her style still remained impressive to critics. In 1967 Neville Braybrooke said that, "her books and stories show the assured touch of a master."[21] Reviews of her earlier work, reprinted after *Wide Sargasso Sea*, show that, by the 1960s, Rhys's work was being read by more critics who were able to understand what she was doing.[22]

Wide Sargasso Sea came out in 1966 and was generally praised by reviewers, but there was an immediate concern that it might be too close to *Jane Eyre*. Though most reviewers thought that it stood, alone, Walter Allen, an influential voice, argued in the *New York Times Book Review* that, despite much that was effective in the novel, "Rochester" is not sufficiently clearly drawn as a character, and the novel is too dependent on Brontë.[23] This was an anxiety in the sixties but, as postcolonial criticism began to seriously notice the way postcolonial writers were "writing back" to British canonical texts, Rhys once more found herself praised in a new era for what she had been doing ahead of her time. John Thieme, in an essay published in 1979, the year of Rhys's death, concluded that Rhys had done a good job of "writing back" to Charlotte Brontë, even to the extent of reflecting the imagery of *Jane Eyre*.[24] In 1993 David Cowart found Rhys's gloss on *Jane Eyre* a "displacing myth" (and therefore modernist), but also "symbiotic," and therefore postmodern as well.[25] Of course this means that the reader who has not read *Jane Eyre* will miss a good deal of Rhys's purpose in *Wide Sargasso Sea*.

After the huge success of *Wide Sargasso Sea*, and the media spin that mythologized Rhys (as a "dead" writer come to life, a siren, an exotic), the volume of Rhys criticism grew enormously. Neville Braybrooke, whose response to Rhys was consistently positive and insightful, reviewed *Wide Sargasso Sea* very favorably, and a few years later (1970) wrote an essay in *Caribbean Quarterly* that related her characterization of women to the nature of white Creoles in Caribbean society. In 1972, he did a piece on her for a book on recent novelists.[26] The same year, Laurence Cole brought back the old objection to her themes, arguing they would keep her readers limited.[27] Elgin Mellown proposed (also in 1972) that all her protagonists are essentially the same woman, an argument that would haunt Rhys criticism for a long time.[28] V. S. Naipaul, the eminent West Indian writer, argued that she was far ahead of her time when he reviewed the reprint of *After Leaving Mr. Mackenzie* in 1972. His support was important to Rhys herself because he was, like her, a transnational writer, with Caribbean origins.[29]

Two years later, in 1974, three major strands of Rhys criticism were becoming evident. A. Alvarez's famous summation in the influential *New York Times Book Review* that Rhys was the best living English novelist ignored her Caribbean identity, which made her rather a fiction writer who worked in English.[30] The Jamaican novelist John Hearne declared Wilson Harris and Jean Rhys to be the two most important West Indian writers of fiction.[31] This was a bold choice, since George Lamming, Austin Clarke,

Samuel Selvon or V. S. Naipaul (to say nothing of Paule Marshall, from the diaspora) might also have been given such a title. By naming Rhys, Hearne gave her important Caribbean literary approval. This was the more significant since her absence from the region for so many years, and her choice of London or Paris as locales for all but two of her novels, meant that some in the region felt she was not really a Caribbean novelist at all. On the feminist side, Nancy J. Casey's exploration of the "liberated woman" in "Temps Perdi" and "I Spy a Stranger" read Rhys as engaged with male domination of women and women betraying other women, both important political foci of what was called the "women's liberation movement" in the 1970's.[32] In 1976, Judith Thurman's essay in the feminist magazine *MS* considered the nature of Rhys's female protagonists, and is interesting in preferring *Good Morning, Midnight* over *Wide Sargasso Sea*, on feminist grounds.[33]

Postcolonial interest in Rhys also began in the late 1970's. The Indian writer Eunice de Souza preferred Rhys to Ruth Prawer Jhabwala because Rhys, "though English herself," did not seek to find favor with the English by caricaturing other races.[34] Helen Tiffin argued that Rhys's female/male, West Indian/English dichotomies reflect a master/slave and colonist/colonized relationship. This claim is somewhat like Gayatri Spivak's, in 1985, that Rhys's *Wide Sargasso Sea* is allegorical, telling the story of the violent relation between colonizer and colonized. Though both are early postcolonial readings of Rhys in tune with the concerns of the late seventies, they now seem very reductive.[35] Postcolonial criticism and theory, whilst offering important overviews of an enormously complicated and various world impacted by colonialism, has at times been tempted to create broad schema that dissolve the intricate interrelation of a particular text with its specific cultural location in space and time.[36]

Late 1970's criticism was also continuing to try to place Rhys's work in relation to modernism and other literary currents of the early twentieth century. In this regard, Todd Bender's article on Rhys and impressionism (1978) is particularly interesting.[37] This thought about Ford Madox Ford's 1924 reading of Conrad as a structural guide for Rhys as she was starting out. The innovative perspective here was the idea that Rhys learned to use deliberately ambiguous tactics to draw in the reader to fill in the gaps (such as narration which could not be trusted or which switched points of view). Bender is correct in pointing out how much Rhys depends on the careful reader who picks up nuances in the telling of the tale and deliberately considers them.

Books on Rhys began to appear in 1978. Louis James's study of Rhys was written at the suggestion of Jamaican poet and critic Mervyn Morris.[38] Like several early Rhys critics, James clearly accepted Rhys's version of her birthdate (he says Rhys was sixteen in 1910, when she was actually twenty). From that error, he calculates that she left Dominica for London in 1910 (she actually left in 1907). He also states that her first husband was Max Hamer, an error repeated twice.[39] But, brief as this book is, James does give a good sense of Rhys's origins in Dominica and her key creative contexts, such as Paris. He also realized the important of the music hall in her work:"She took over its juxtaposition of fantasy and tawdry reality: she used its motifs and rhythms to orchestrate her fiction."[40]

Early scholars of Rhys were all led astray by her declaration of her date of birth, even when they were careful in other respects. Thomas Staley (whose book on Rhys appeared in the year of her death) was the agency who made possible the acquisition of the Rhys papers for the University of Tulsa. He repeats the errors of the 1894 birthdate and the 1910 leaving of Dominica, and dismisses the music hall as proving a "tawdry show-business world of the also-rans" for Rhys[41] This judgment ignores the strong characters she drew from it, such as Maudie and Laurie in *Voyage in the Dark*, as well as the role of popular song in her work overall. But he pays close attention to the development of Rhys as a modernist and his sense of what Rhys brought to her contemporary literary world (or ignored in it) is acute. He is aware of the way Rhys introduced something new by depicting women outside the protected world of the middle class so central, for example, to the work of Virginia Woolf, and he makes a thoughtful comparison between Rhys and the French writer Colette, finding it hard to see a direct influence from Colette but also rightly seeing the two as productively read together. Peter Wolfe (1980) tries to link Rhys's life and work (something not easy to do well, and Wolfe had limited biographical resources). He repeats the same errors of fact with regard to her birthdate and date of leaving Dominica and also says that in *Wide Sargasso Sea* Pierre is killed as the house burns, whereas he died on the journey away from the burning house.[42] Arnold Davidson (1985) rested a good deal on a biographical reading of Rhys, but got her birthdate and the date she left Dominica correct.[43] He thinks *Wide Sargasso Sea* is her "socially most important book,"[44] but he does understand the complexity of *Good Morning, Midnight.*

Opening a decade in which much feminist criticism on Rhys appeared, Helen Nebeker's *Jean Rhys: Woman in Passage* (1981) uses mythology and psychology. But it forces Rhys into a side-current of feminist politics: Nebeker reads the name Anna in *Voyage in the Dark* quite wrong-headedly as reflective of Sumerian, Graeco-Roman, Celtic and Hebrew constructions of a powerful goddess/priestess, something Nebeker says shows Rhys "subliminally playing upon unconscious racial memories."[45] She also accepted the common assumption that Rhys was born in 1894. Elizabeth Baer's essay on the "sisterhood" of Jane Eyre and Antoinette Cosway takes a key feminist concept and uses it interestingly to read the madwoman Bertha's warning to Jane Eyre from the attic as the reason Eyre defers marriage to Rochester until he no longer is her superior. She also offers an excellent reading of the three dreams Antoinette has in *Wide Sargasso Sea.*[46] Whilst responsible and interesting, Nancy Harrison's *Jean Rhys and the Novel as Women's Text* seems dated now in its desire to define a female-authored text as requiring a female audience (now the complicated nature of gender is far more likely to inform close readings that think about cultural politics around sexually determined role-playing). But she has a thought-provoking chapter on "Rochester" 's narrative in *Wide Sargasso Sea.* In this she extends an argument made earlier in the book about the role of a "mother-text" in Rhys's fiction to the idea of a "father-text" as well. She reads "Rochester" 's story as suppressing his mother, and therefore his own "mother-text."[47] In *The Unspeakable Mother*, Deborah Kelly Kloepfer, compares Rhys to the remarkable modernist poet H. D. in productive and groundbreaking ways.[48] Kloepfer also writes out of the moment when French and English feminist theory was frequently opposed, French being generally defined as theoretical and English as politically activist. She references Julia Kristeva's work on the mother as ambiguous symbol to centrally inform her work on Rhys, beginning from the important fact of Rhys's tensions with her own mother from childhood on. Other feminist studies from this era that include Rhys include Judith Kegan Gardiner's *Rhys, Stead, Lessing and the Politics of Empathy*, which is again interested in the mother in Rhys's work, and Molly Hite's *The Other Side of the Story.*[49] Hite begins by noting that, in the eighties, feminist critics replaced the formalist emphasis of 1970's work on Rhys by integrating discussion of Rhys's life and her work, and usefully insists that Rhys's work resists ideological readings because of the destabilizing marginality of her protagonists.

Culture wars were going on in the Caribbean just as Rhys's *Wide Sargasso Sea* became well known and she gradually became a metaphor in important defining debates. In 1968, Wally Look Lai discussed the importance of *Wide Sargasso Sea* as a West Indian novel. He read the ending, as Antoinette dreams of jumping from the roof of the burning house, calling Tia's name, a return home.[50] The Trinidadian critic Kenneth Ramchand included Rhys in his seminal *The West Indian Novel and Its Background*, in a chapter on white Creoles organized around Fanon's "terrified consciousness."[51] The 1970's were a period of turbulence in the Caribbean, where positions on race, culture and the direction the region should go were intensely debated. The major critic and historian Kamau Brathwaite published his theory of Caribbean culture in the mid-seventies. In this he explained that "creolization is a process that relates to dominant and sub-dominant groups." He noted that metropolitan critics had been impressed with *Wide Sargasso Sea*, that Ramchand had called white fear "universal," and that Look Lai had emphasized the relation between Creole and metropole. All these affirmed for Brathwaite that Rhys as a white Creole writer was accepted by the dominant racial group, whites, in Britain.[52] But, for Brathwaite, whatever Antoinette hopes and dreams in the last moments of her life, she could not actually jump to join Tia because, given the racial history of the region, that could only be fantasy. He thought both Look Lai and Ramchand projected an optimistic/universalistic view with regard to Rhys.[53] Brathwaite's position provoked a number of responses and discussions, such as O'Callaghan's defense of early white women writers in the Caribbean.[54] In an exchange with Peter Hulme on the same topic, in the mid-1990's, Brathwaite inventively called Rhys "The Helen of our Wars."[55] The theme of race in Rhys criticism also appears in the work of Maggie Humm and Jean d'Costa.[56]

A number of detailed and nuanced Caribbean-centered studies emerged in the 1990s, such as the work of Veronica Gregg and Judith Raiskin.[57] Gregg, a Jamaican critic, thoughtfully considers the culture wars around Rhys and points out that Rhys's imagination is "profoundly racialized, even racist,"[58] but also that her Creole identity has to be examined not only in terms of "reading" but in terms of Rhys's performance of Creole writing. Raiskin argues that Rhys's white Creole perspective "challenges the geneticist concept of race by exploring the relationship of racial categories to power and culture."[59] Karin Williamson (1986) offers a careful comparison of the two significant white female Creole Dominican writers, Rhys and Phyllis Shand Allfrey, which establishes a number of interesting textual correlations.[60] Carolyn Vellenga Berman more recently (2006) begins from a reading of the English domestic novel, in the context of the battle to end slavery. Her chapter on *Wide Sargasso Sea* affirms that Rhys's project is to vindicate Creoles (by which Rhys means white West Indians).[61]

Wilson Harris, the major Guyanese writer, delivered a lecture in 1980 called "Carnival of Psyche: Jean Rhys's *Wide Sargasso Sea*," in which he offered a reading of Rhys in the frame of his own theory of Caribbean (and Americas) culture, which is highly mytho-poetic and deeply innovative.[62] He takes as his starting point Antoinette's vision of the "tree of life in flames" at the end of *Wide Sargasso Sea:* this is the flamboyant tree which is key in Amerindian legend in the Caribbean.

Rhys has also been fortunate to have meticulous scholars investigate key details in her work. Of recent postcolonial perspectives, Peter Hulme's scholarship on Carib culture in Dominica, as well as his painstaking work on Rhys's adaptation of the dates of the story of Bertha in *Jane Eyre* and her use of her own family history in the novel, offer fascinating insights into Rhys's likely imaginative sources and her process.[63] The work of Mary Lou Emery (1990) meticulously and subtly explores the cultural spaces in Rhys's texts. Moira Ferguson (1993) reads *Wide Sargasso Sea* in conjunction with other women writers, including Mary Wollstonecraft and Jane Austen, in an important exploration of gender and colonialism.[64] Sue Thomas's *The Worlding of Jean Rhys* thoroughly examines Rhys's engagement with social currents around her, paying close attention to Rhys's fictional process from notebooks to finished texts. Thomas discusses social issues which Rhys indirectly challenged or addressed in her work. Amongst these are the "panic" in Britain about "amateur prostitution" in the early twentieth century and the anxiety around obeah in the Dominica of Rhys's childhood.[65] More recently, Carine Mardorossian answers the charge, by Gregg and others, that Rhys marginalizes black subjectivity in her work by calling on Edouard Glissant's idea of "opacity" (the reluctance of anti-colonial culture to facilitate colonial knowledge of it) and by reading it alongside Maryse Condé's *Windward Heights* (1998).[66]

Coral Ann Howells (1991) stressed three constructions of Rhys's writerly identity as being connected; woman, colonial, modernist.[67] My own *Jean Rhys*, seven years after Howells, sought to demonstrate how deeply the Caribbean informs all of her work, and inevitably also stressed the cultural and political complexity of it.[68] More recently, Carol Dell'Amico's *Colonialism and the Modern Movement in the Early Novels of Jean Rhys* connects the colonial and the modern in her work.[69]

Rhys is now canonical. There are overviews of her work and anthologies of Rhys criticism,[70] and both a reader's guide to criticism on *Wide Sargasso Sea* and the Norton edition of *Wide Sargasso Sea*.[71] Helen Carr's useful profile is a title in a series, Writers and their Work.[72] The journal *Jean Rhys Review* became a resource for scholars from 1987, founded by Nora Gaines.[73] Rhys's work is a staple in literature courses in tertiary education. Like Hemmerecht's structuralist study, others, such as those of Le Gallez and Burrowes, began as doctoral dissertations.[74] Bibliographical resources, most notably Mellown (1984) and Paravisini-Gebert and Torres-Seda (1993) facilitate Rhys research, though there is a constant need of updating.[75]

Carole Angier's biography, *Jean Rhys*, is a mixed blessing, but undeniably useful. Rhys left instructions that no biography of her was to be written.

Though Angier irresponsibly often used the work to read gaps in the life, for which she received justifiable negative criticism, she also did an excellent job of dismissing some persistent Rhys myths. Her access to key figures in Rhys's life was in the nick of time, given their age, and though her research into Dominica and Paris could have been much stronger, her careful exploration of Rhys's lost years in Britain is particularly useful. Other biographical sources include the self-admitted memoirish books by former *Granta* editor and friend of Rhys Alexis Lykiard, *Jean Rhys Revisited* and *Jean Rhys Afterwards.*[76]

But it is important to note that, when there is extensive interest in a writer, there is also likely to be hasty, inaccurate and misleading criticism. Rhys has attracted, for the most part, outstanding critics, but the reader should be also be careful. For example, she is included in the opportunistic *Great Women Writers* (1990), an ambitious anthology intended for women's studies survey courses.[77] Among the numerous errors in the essay on Rhys, 1894 is given as her birthdate (unforgivable in 1994); and it is claimed that she played "a noteworthy role in the Left Bank literary scene" (she was always a loner), that her mother was "part-Creole" and Rhys was thought "colored" in England, and that the growth of interest in her work came only from the feminist movement (the rise of interest in postcolonial themes and her aesthetics has clearly been as important and will probably have more longevity). In addition, an unexamined acceptance of *Wide Sargasso Sea* as Rhys's best work is hopefully unlikely to be made in the future. This judgment occurs in studies by both Arnold Davidson (1985) and Sanford Sternlicht (1997).[78] Another critical pitfall is making reductive and unreliable readings of Rhys's intentions, such as Sternlicht's unfortunate assertion that alienation in *Good Morning, Midnight* may be the way Rhys "surfaced her repressed anger" because she was ignored by the British *literati.*[79] Psychoanalytic approaches to Rhys have drawn on Freud and Lacan, in terms of the family dramas in Rhys's texts and the key role of the mirror in her work. Anne Simpson's recent study, *Territories of the Psyche*, points out that Freudian analyses are generally male-centered but mother–child relations are central to Rhys's texts. But readers are warned that such approaches tend to make Rhys follow their own paradigms: Simpson disturbingly talks about what she thinks Rhys may have gained therapeutically from writing her fiction.[80]

As for the present and future of Rhys studies, it looks as if new perspectives will continue to emerge. It is likely that more European studies of her work will appear. Those already in print include Tarozzi (1984), Hemmerechts (1987), Joubert (1997) and Yoris-Villasana (2004).[81]

Comparative studies of Rhys and other writers have helped complicate perceptions of her work and cultural location. Lorna Sage's *Women in the House of Fiction* (1992) examines French, British and US writers including Simone de Beauvoir, Doris Lessing, Toni Morrison and Rhys: she calls Rhys "the post-war writer as ghost."[82] Ileana Rodriguez, in *House/Garden/Nation* (1994), discusses Rhys within her postcolonial reading of Latin American literature by women, in which she reads "Rochester"'s "derangement" in the context of magical realism.[83] Also comparative criticism of Caribbean writers often includes substantial discussion of Rhys. Belinda Edmondson, in *Making Men* (1999), thoughtfully combines gender and Caribbean-centered criticism and reads Rhys alongside Michelle Cliff and Jamaica Kincaid. Margaret Paul Joseph, in *Caliban in Exile* (1992), explores Shakespeare's Caliban as outsider in relation to Rhys, Selvon and Lamming. Leah Rosenberg's *Nationalism and the Formation of Caribbean Literature* (2007) includes a chapter on Rhys's work which locates her in relation to other Caribbean writers of the 1920s and 1930s and thoughtfully comments on Rhys's often problematic construction of race, as well as her complicated sense of her own racial and cultural location. Avril Horner and Sue Zlosnik, in *Landscapes of Desire* (1990), read three of her novels (out of chronological order) in a volume alongside Edith Wharton, Charlotte Perkins Gilman, Kate Chopin, Virginia Woolf and Margaret Atwood. Erica L. Johnson, in *Home, Maison, Casa* (2003) reads Rhys with Marguerite Dumas and Erminia Dell'Oro, with the theme of the "politics of location."[84] It is also probable (and desirable) that Rhys should be compared to other women writers who were or are out of place, in a sense, such as Ruth Prawer Jhabvala or Olive Schreiner (the latter comparison implicitly occurs in Raiskin's *Snow on the Canefields*). It is clear that studies of Rhys's use of popular culture are a coming area of scholarly interest.

Rhys's short stories have received much less attention than her novels, but comparative studies of her stories along with those of other masters of this genre, such as Hemingway, Colette or Joyce, would enable valuable new readings of her short fiction to emerge. Charles May never mentions Rhys in his recent survey of the short story.[85] But he points out that though the short story has ancient roots it came into its own as modernism developed in Europe, because it is well suited to the portrayal of the outsider, reacting to or participating in a divided society. Rhys's great theme in her fiction is the outsider and her short stories are no exception. Nor do many of Rhys's stories quite fit into the predominantly realist (naturalistic and direct) tradition of the West Indian short story as defined by Stewart Brown, yet she has an ability to make the gritty details of life's material necessities a key part of even the most Gothic of her tales.[86]

Finally, a little-noted but important aspect of the reception of Rhys's work lies in the numerous Caribbean writers who respect and admire her work enough to let it influence theirs, as in Margaret Cezair-Thompson's *The True History of Paradise* (1999) or Robert Antoni's *Blessed is the fruit* (1997), or to make her a subject of it as Derek Walcott, Lorna Goodison and Olive Senior do in their poems.[87]

Notes

Chapter 1 Life

1 Carole Angier, *Jean Rhys*, Boston, MA: Little, Brown, 1990, 9–11.
2 Lennox Honychurch, *The Dominica Story: A History of the Island*, Roseau, Dominica: The Dominica Institute, 1984, 11, 113.
3 Ibid., 117, 119.
4 See Madison Smartt Bell, *Toussaint Louverture: A Biography*, New York: Pantheon Books, 2000.
5 Honychurch, *Dominica Story*, 98–104.
6 Angier, *Jean Rhys.*, 7.
7 The Lockharts were not unusual in denying the possibility of interracial inheritance in their family.
8 Honychurch, *Dominica Story*, 98–104.
9 Also for Bell, see Peter Hulme, *Remnants of Conquest: The Island Caribs and Their Visitors, 1877–1998*, Oxford: Oxford University Press, 2000, 97–154.
10 Dominican newspapers such as the *Dominica Dial* are on microfiche in the Colindale collection of the British Library in London. See Sue Thomas, *The Worlding of Jean Rhys*, Westport: Greenwood Press, 1999 10–11; also Irving W. Andre, *Distant Voices: The Genesis of an Indigenous Literature in Dominica*, Brampton, Ontario: Pond Casse Press, 1995.
11 Angier, *Jean Rhys*, 8–9, 10. For much more on Williams, see Sue Thomas, "William Rees Williams in Dominica," *Jean Rhys Review*, vol. 7, nos. 1 & 2, 3–14; also the Dominican newspaper, *Dominica Dial*, May 31, 1884, August 30, 1884, November 29, 1884. For related contexts, Lizabeth Paravisini-Gebert, *Phyllis Shand Allfrey: A Caribbean Life*, New Brunswick: Rutgers University Press, 1996.
12 The house Rhys lived in as a child still stands in Roseau. The Bona Vista estate house no longer exists, but ruined fragments identify the site.
13 Honychurch, *Dominica Story*, 96.
14 Ford Madox Ford, "Preface" to Jean Rhys, *The Left Bank*, London: Jonathan Cape, 1927, 24.
15 Though Angier (*Jean Rhys*, 32–3) speculates about this, Hulme (*Remnants*, 222n) dismisses it as fantasy.
16 There are four major notebooks in the Rhys Collection at the Mcfarlin Library, University of Tulsa, identified, respectively, as The Black, Red, Green and Orange

Exercise Books. See Teresa O'Connor, *Jean Rhys: The West Indian Novels*, New York: New York University Press, 1986, 25–6 for Howard.

17 Angier, *Jean Rhys*, 45–53.

18 Ibid, 49.

19 Ibid., 62–8.

20 Diana Athill, Introduction to Jean Rhys, *Smile Please: An Unfinished Autobiography*, Berkeley: Donald S. Ellis, 1979, 7.

21 Rhys's guarded version in *SP*, 92–4 should be compared with Angier's (*Jean Rhys*, 71–9). Angier problematically relies a good deal on Rhys's unpublished novel, "Triple Sec," and *Voyage in the Dark* for her account of this period.

22 See Angier, *Jean Rhys*, 80–97.

23 Martien Kappers-den Hollander, "Jean Rhys and the Dutch Connection," *Maatstaf*, 30 (1982), 30–40; reprinted in *Journal of Modern Literature*, vol. 11, no. 1 (March 1984), 159–83.

24 Angier, *Jean Rhys*, 123–4. This is again speculative.

25 Arthur Mizener sums up Ford thus: "if he neither was not nor thought of himself the greatest writer of his time, he was nonetheless a superbly talented man" (*The Saddest Story: A Biography of Ford Madox Ford*, New York: Carroll and Graf, 1971, xxi).

26 Stella Bowen, *Drawn from Life*, London: Virago (1941), 1984, 166. Also eds. Sondra J. Stang and Karen Cochran, *The Correspondence of Ford Madox Ford and Stella Bowen*, Bloomington: Indiana University Press, 1993, xiv, 260, 312.

27 See also Ford's introduction to Rhys's first book, *The Left Bank*, in which he talks about how he encouraged Rhys to add in local color, or description of place, but she resisted, just as young French writers, her contemporaries, were resisting "the descriptive passage," "Preface," 25.

28 Angier, *Jean Rhys*, 126, 133.

29 Though in 1928 the translation was credited to Ford, because his publisher thought the book would sell better that way, Rhys has received credit since (Francis Carco, *Perversity*, Berkeley: Black Lizard Books, 1987). See Angier, *Jean Rhys*, 164. Both Rhys and Ford had a transnational, multilingual background and experience.

30 Ford Madox Ford, *When the Wicked Man*, New York: Horace Liveright, Inc: 1931, 267. Carole Ohman (*Ford Madox Ford: From Apprentice to Craftsman*, Middletown, CT: Wesleyan University Press, 1964, 178) rightly points to the "oversimplified and hurried statement" by which Ford delineates character in this novel.

31 Angier, *Jean Rhys*, 231.

32 Ibid., 129–130; 287–290.

33 See Kappers-den Hollander, "Dutch Connection."

34 Angier, *Jean Rhys*, 371.

35 Ibid., 436–7. The Sachsenhausen death march was an attempt by Nazi Germany to hide evidence of the Holocaust as it was clear they were going to lose the war.

36 Ibid., 435.

37 Ibid., 456–7, 464.
38 Ibid., 450–4.
39 Ibid., 460.
40 Ibid., 475.
41 Ibid., 481–3.
42 Ibid., 521, 523.
43 Ibid., 652–3.

Chapter 2 Contexts

1 Angela Leighton reports that Hemans was deserted by her husband and had five sons to rear, and earned a living from her writing of poetry to which women readers responded in the 1820s and 1830s: her need to write for money was cited as her chief failing with regard to the quality of her work. The title Mrs. Hemans was one that appealed to younger women (*Victorian Women Poets: Writing Against the Heart*, Charlottesville: University Press of Virginia, 1992, 10–11, 14, 16).
2 Guy de Maupassant (1850–93) was a popular French naturalistic novelist and story writer. He wrote six novels. *Fort Comme La Mort* – as Rhys gives the title – (1889) is not one of his best works.
3 Ford Madox Ford, "Preface", to Jean Rhys, *The Left Bank*, London: Jonathan Cape, 1927, 24.
4 D. B. Wyndham-Lewis, "Hinterland of Bohemia," *Saturday Review*, 143 (April 23, 1927), 637; A. Alvarez, *New York Times Book Review*, March 17, 1974, 6–7. See also Kenneth Ramchand, *The West Indian Novel and Its Background*, London: Heineman (1970), 1983. Ramchand cites *Wide Sargasso Sea*'s publication as the beginning of English attention to white West Indian writing (223).
5 Malcolm Bradbury and James McFarlane have an image that aptly sums up this process of modernity, "something that progresses in company with and at the speed of the years, like the bow-wave of a ship; last year's modern is not this year's," in eds. Malcolm Bradbury and James McFarlane, *Modernism 1890–1930*, Harmondsworth: Penguin, 1976, 22.
6 Modernism often interweaves strategies from different art forms or different aspects of the same art, which can suggest effective ways of reading a modernist text. Jewel Spears Brooker and Joseph Bentley make the analogy between a modernist text and a musical score in *Reading The Waste Land: Modernism and the Limits of Interpretation*, Amherst: University of Massachussetts Press, 1990, 8.
7 However, Louis Menand and Lawrence Rainey's otherwise excellent introduction to a definitive volume on modernist criticism omits all mention of the study and assessment of literary modernisms outside Europe and the USA, perhaps because they feel that it is risky for professional literary studies to be "animated by political ambitions," at odds with "the sympathies of even the liberal and well-educated public" (Introduction, *The Cambridge History of Literary Criticism*,

Vol. VII, *Modernism and the New Criticism*, Cambridge: Cambridge University Press, 2000, 3). But cultural differences are key in considering modernisms. European culture often expresses the reaction of an individual to a changing environment. In postcolonial cultures, collectivity was and is related to traditions suppressed by colonial intrusion, but at the same time European emphasis on individuality was inculcated by colonial education. Complex forms of literary expression such as magical realism have evolved to express these dynamics, produced by such writers as Garcia Marquez, Salman Rushdie, Kamau Brathwaite and, more recently, Robert Antoni. Their work stretches the boundaries of modernism and even expresses a postmodern sense of multiple selves.

8 See Franz Kuna, "Vienna and Prague 1890–1928" (in eds, Bradbury and McFarlane, *Modernism*, 120–33). Rhys was certainly in Vienna just after the First World War, and possibly in Prague (Carole Angier, *Jean Rhys*, Boston, MA: Little, Brown, 121). Kuna reminds us that these two cities "spawned some of the major writers of the age (Hofmannsthal, Schnitzler, Rilke, Kafka, Musil)," as well as composers, and of course Freud (Vienna) (120).

9 An obvious parallel with Rhys in this is Virginia Woolf (1882–1941).

10 See Sue Thomas, *The Worlding of Jean Rhys*, Westport: Greenwood Press, 1999 136–7 for a discussion of the image of the machine in *Good Morning, Midnight*; also Mary Lou Emery, *Jean Rhys at "World's End": Novels of Colonial and Sexual Exile*, Austin: University of Texas Press, 1990, 167 for a discussion of the same topic and text.

11 Emery, *World's End*, 175. Emery points out that Rhys's "shifting and dissolving narrative point of view" and "circularity and repetition" are connected to themes of possession and dispossession and "zombie life-in-death and death-in-life" which are deeply connected to the Caribbean.

12 Ford, "Preface," 24.

13 This story originally appeared in *Tigers are Better-Looking* and so was completed late in her career.

14 This was Ford's celebrated modernist literary journal, of which he wrote in the first edition that its aim was to help do away with national literatures: "there will be only Literature" (Alan Judd, *Ford Madox Ford*, London: Harper Collins, 1991, 345). Hemingway would not only be published in the journal but helped edit it. Rhys was consistent in her interest in the connection between culture and power. Ford pulled off the coup of publishing an extract from Joyce's *Finnegans Wake* (ibid., 348).

15 "Tradition and the Individual Talent" went through some revisions in its early publication history, so it is dated 1917, 1919, and 1920 in various sources. *The Sacred Wood: Essays on Poetry and Criticism* (London: Methuen, 1920) included it.

16 National boundaries dissolved for this coterie of male literary talent, many of whom traveled widely and lived away from home, or communicated beyond their main creative base. W.B. Yeats told Ezra Pound about Joyce, and Pound then enabled the publication of some of Joyce's work. Pound met Eliot in London in 1914 and provided excellent editorial advice for Eliot.

17 Paul Foster, *The Golden Lotus: Buddhist Influence in T. S.Eliot's Four Quartets*, Sussex: The Book Guild, 1998.

18 Coral Ann Howells (*Jean Rhys*, New York: St Martin's Press, 1991, 99–100) notes particularly the mocking of Joyce's Molly Bloom in the voice of Sasha in *Good Morning, Midnight*, as well as the echoes of the typist and Tiresias in Eliot's *The Waste Land.*

19 Judith Thurman, "Introduction," *Colette: Chéri and The Last of Chéri*, New York: Farrar, Straus and Giroux, 2001, xi. *Chéri* appeared in 1919, just as Rhys was settling into her first marriage in Paris and Europe, and just a few years before her writing career began. *The Last of Chéri* appeared in 1926, before Rhys's first book was published.

20 I am grateful to Nora Gaines, former editor of the *Jean Rhys Review*, for pointing this out. Judith Thurman (*A Life of Colette*, New York: Ballantine Books, 1999) comments on this text (much as we could comment on Rhys's *Smile Please*), "even if we don't accept *My Apprenticeships* as the truth, we should accept it as Colette's truth" (65).

21 Colette published a great number of stories between 1908 and 1945, which like Rhys's fall into different subgroups. Robert Phelps (ed., *The Collected Stories of Colette*, New York: Farrar, Straus and Giroux, 1983, xv) lists these as including personal reportage, autobiographical sketches, lyrical meditations and short stories with character, dialogue and plot. Comparison of Rhys's stories with those of Colette is very rewarding and suggests that Rhys may have had some inspiration from Colette's accounts of the consciousness of a hat-shop saleswoman, a corset-maker, a hairdresser, a masseuse or a scene in a bar, all in Paris. Colette's breathless collage of impressions and lively snippets of dialogue certainly parallel Rhys's own aesthetic in her early stories as well as her novels.

22 Colette, *The Pure and the Impure*, trans. Herma Briffault, London: Secker and Warburg, 1968.

23 Ford, "Preface," 27.

24 Nancy Harrison, *Jean Rhys and the Novel as Women's Text*, Chapel Hill: University of North Carolina Press, 1988, 44.

25 Caroline Rody, *The Daughter's Return: African-American and Caribbean Women's Fictions of History*, Oxford: Oxford University Press, 2001, 135. Rhys was both critical and admiring of Brontë (*L*:271)

26 Paula Le Gallez, *The Rhys Woman* (New York: St Martin's Press, 1990), speaks of Rhys's "implicit feminism" (6).

27 Sidonie Smith, *A Poetics of Women's Autobiography: Marginality and the Fictions of Self-Representation*, Bloomington: Indiana University Press, 1987, 52.

28 Declan Kiberd, *Inventing Ireland: The Literature of the Modern Nation*, London: Vintage, 1996, 326, 339.

29 See Michael Echeruo, *Joyce Cary and the Novel of Africa*, London: Longman, 1973 and Robert M. Wren, *Achebe's World: The Historical and Cultural Context of the Novels of Chinua Achebe*, Burnt Mill, Essex: Longman, 1980.

30 See ed. Daryl Cumber Dance, *Fifty Caribbean Writers*, Westport, CT: Greenwood Press, 1986, for bio-bibliographical essays on these writers.

31 Hesketh Bell, *Glimpses of a Governor's Life*, London: Sampson, Low, Marston & Co., 1946, 22.

32 Evelyn O'Callaghan, *Women Writing the West Indies, 1804–1939, "A Hot Place Belonging to Us"*, New York: Routledge, 2004, argues that it is important to read pro-colonial white women writers, even if not born in the Caribbean, to see what kind of agency their writing had in dispersing their beliefs. See also, for an account of Rhys's sense of her own white Caribbean identity, David Plante, *Difficult Women*, New York: Dutton, 1984.

33 Robert Antoni, *Blessed is the fruit*, New York: Henry Holt, 1997.

34 Version 7 is the only one with a date (24 March, 1974). In the mid-seventies, Rhys was working on her volume of short stories titled *Sleep It Off Lady* (1976). "The Bishop's Feast" in that collection was originally part of "The Imperial Road" (Version 1). Angier points out that many of the stories in this collection were first in draft in the 1930's and that an early draft of *Wide Sargasso Sea* was completed before 1940. This story was rejected because it was thought racially insensitive, "anti-Negro." See, for a discussion of the likely last version, Elaine Savory, "The Text and the World: Jean Rhys's 'The Imperial Road,'" *Jean Rhys Review*, vol. 11, no. 2, 4–16.

35 Hannah Carter, "Fated to be Sad," *Guardian*, Thursday August 5, 1968, 5.

Chapter 3 Texts

1 The French writer Francis Carco (1886–1956) was, like Rhys, an outsider on several levels. He was born on a small island, New Caledonia, a Pacific French colony, to Corsican parents. Like her, he wrote about bohemian life in Montmartre. "Tout Montparnasse and a Lady" is set in a *bal musette*. "Musette" is both a modern cultural invention comparable to jazz, and associated particularly with Paris, and an instrument called the musette, similar to bagpipes.

2 The name William signified Jean Lenglet (Willem), William Rees Williams, Rhys's father, and one of Rhys's brothers. Owen was the name of another brother. (Carole Angier, *Jean Rhys*, Boston, MA: Little, Brown, 1990. 9, 103, 112). Rhys's representations of her protagonists' family ties are far less normatively affectionate.

3 Ford Madox Ford, "Preface" to Jean Rhys, *The Left Bank*, London: Jonathan Cape, 1927, 25–6.

4 Angier, *Jean Rhys*, 139.

5 Ibid., 177.

6 *Quartet* was made into a film (Merchant/Ivory, 1981). For issues around the numerous dramatizations of Rhys's work, see Angier, *Jean Rhys*, 500–1, 580.

7 Pastoral is a literary convention, originating in ancient Greece, and highly influential in canonical English literature. The shepherd with his pipe is equated

with the original making of poetry (verbal music) in an idyllic setting. Pastoral is often nostalgic, or at least somewhat escapist. Rhys's down-to-earth use of it is thus deliciously nuanced.

8 Eliot's "Little Gidding" was an Anglican community established in 1625, in Huntingdonshire (Britain), which protected Charles I after an important defeat in the Civil War. It thus resonated for Eliot as a place where Anglicans had made common cause with Catholics to oppose the Puritans during the English Civil War. See Denis Donoghue, *Words Alone: The Poet T. S. Eliot*, New Haven: Yale University Press, 2000, 278.

9 The Lenglets, Ella and Jean, lived in the Rue Lamartine, in Montmartre, twice, returning in 1922 (Angier, *Jean Rhys*, 122). Ford and Bowen at one point lived in an apartment in the Rue Denfert-Rochereau in 1924. Thus Rhys really does recreate an emotional geography of those years.

10 I have retained Rhys's double accent, although "Médecine" is more familiar.

11 Joseph Conrad, 1857–1924, born in the Ukraine to Polish parents, late a naturalized Briton. *Almayer's Folly: The Story of an Eastern River* (1895) was an apprentice work. Its Almayer is a Dutch trader in Borneo in the late 1800s. In its themes of desire for riches, colonialism, race and sex and slavery, it clearly speaks to Norah's concerns.

12 Rather than the usual anglicized spelling of Dostoyevsky.

13 This group of friends conducted regular meetings after about 1906, and included not only the Woolfs, but many other distinguished and well-educated people such as Lytton Strachey, E. M. Forster and John Maynard Keynes.

14 Established in 1865 in Regent Street, the Café Royal was made famous by Oscar Wilde when he made it his favorite place to hold court.

15 It is useful to recall that Rhys translated Carco's novel *Perversion*; the reference thus probably critiques the thrills of fashionable bohemian slumming.

16 Like Rhys, Eliot had a sense of humor about pretentious avante-garde intellectual life, as in his notes on *The Waste Land*, in which he had fun sending off earnest critics and readers to hunt down "meaning."

17 *Voyage in the Dark* is set in 1912–14 (Rhys's affair with Lancelot Grey Hugh Smith was ongoing in 1911). "Triple Sec" is in the Rhys Collection at the University of Tulsa's McFarlin Library.

18 Kincaid's narrative voices in *At the Bottom of the River* (1983) and *Annie John* (1985) speak sparely: they are somewhat reminiscent of Anna's voice. Kincaid's characters are, however, far more strongly self-determined.

19 Zola's central character, Nana, was a metaphor for social ills in French society. A poor prostitute, she rises to become a powerful and longed-for high-class courtesan, but destroys men and finally dies horribly of smallpox. Anna turns out to be entirely unable to destroy men, and is almost destroyed herself. Rhys's deployment of *Nana* (1880) is thus ironic.

20 D'Adhémar has Aubrey Beardsley prints. Beardsley (1872–1895), close to Oscar Wilde, was a very gifted decadent illustrator, whose extremely striking and

elegant black and white drawings were mildly pornographic. Anna's lack of worldliness is displayed in this scene.

21 For Columbus, see Teresa O'Connor, *Jean Rhys: The West Indian Novels*, New York: New York University Press, 1986, 13–14; and for Dominica, see Louis James, *Jean Rhys*, London: Longman, 1978, 1; Peter Hulme, *Remnants of Conquest: The Island Caribs and Their Visitors, 1877–1998*, Oxford: Oxford University Press, 2000, 196–7.

22 Rhys anticipated the use of folk traditions by later Caribbean women novelists such as Merle Hodge, *Crick Crack Monkey* (1970) and Nalo Hopkinson, *Brown Girl in the Ring* (1998).

23 "Kubla Khan" (1797) was a famously anthologized poem in Britain during Rhys's lifetime, loved for its strongly Romantic, lush language and mysteriously fragmentary nature.

24 O'Connor, *West Indian Novels*, 132.

25 Ibid., 137

26 This is more about Walter's cultural pretentiousness than Voltaire, the French philosopher and writer (1694–1778).

27 For a glossary that includes obeah and related terms, see eds. Margarite Fernández Olmos and Lizabeth Paravisini-Gebert, *Sacred Possessions: Vodou, Santería, Obeah and the Caribbean*, New Brunswick: Rutgers University Press, 1997.

28 For a detailed discussion of the horrific exploitation of Bartmann, see Sander Gilman, "Black Bodies, White Bodies: Toward an Iconography of Female Sexuality in Late Nineteenth Century Art, Medicine and Literature," *Critical Inquiry*, vol. 12, no. 1, (Autumn 1985), 204–42.

29 Coral Ann Howells, *Jean Rhys*, New York: St Martin's Press, 1991, 68.

30 Angier, *Jean Rhys*, 7, 357.

31 Kate O'Brien, "Fiction," *Spectator*, 162 (June 16, 1939), 1062.

32 "Good Morning – Midnight –," *The Complete Poems of Emily Dickinson*, ed. Thomas H. Johnson, New York: Little, Brown, 1961, no. 425, p. 203. Dickinson's poems were mainly left in manuscript and have often been intrusively edited. Johnson's edition rightly retreats from that disturbance of what we may assume were her final intentions. Rhys's quotation follows another editorial version.

33 This disconnection is evident in postcolonial culture, reflecting the arbitrariness of power and the refusal of the powerful to communicate well with subordinates.

34 See Sue Thomas, *The Worlding of Jean Rhys*, Westport: Greenwood Press, 1999, 117–20.

35 Oscar Wilde's witty comedy (1892), a perfectly respectable text via which to conduct an English lesson, even if the writer was a subversive bohemian.

36 Howells, *Jean Rhys*, 99, points out that Rhys is writing back to both *Ulysses* and *The Waste Land.*

37 See, for a discussion of this intertextuality, John Thieme, *Postcolonial Con-texts: Writing Back to the Canon*, London: Continuum, 77–85.

38 Angier, *Jean Rhys*, 446–7. This period in the mid-fifties preceded Rhys's sustained application to *Wide Sargasso Sea.*
39 Lennox Honychurch, *The Dominica Story: A History of the Island*, Roseau, Dominica: The Dominica Institute, 1984, 31.
40 See Teresa O'Connor, "Jean Rhys, Paul Theroux and the Imperial Road," *Twentieth Century Literature*, vol. 38, no.4, (Winter 1992), 404–14.
41 Hesketh Bell, in *Glimpses of a Governor's Life*, London: Sampson, Low, Marston & Co., 1946, thought obeah still very powerful among Caribbean people during his time there in Rhys's childhood. Rhys believed one of the servants at Bona Vista to be an obeah woman (*SP*:15). See also Hesketh Bell, *Obeah, Witchcraft in the West Indies*, London: Sampson, Low, Marston, Searle and Rivington, 1889; Thomas, *Worlding*, 157–71.
42 See note. 25. The zombi is made by a powerful magician, using drugs most likely, and then enslaved.
43 Angier, *Jean Rhys*, 446–7.
44 See ibid., 441–8 for details of a difficult period in Rhys's own life, some details of which were reworked for Selina's story.
45 The racial reference is ambiguous, but leads the reader to speculate whether a woman of color would be working on a cruise ship going to South Africa during the apartheid period.
46 Angier, *Jean Rhys*, 429.
47 Wordsworth's "I wandered lonely as a Cloud," with its "host of dancing Daffodils" became notorious during the British Empire when many colonial children who had never seen a daffodil were forced to learn the poem. Kincaid references the way the poem is resented, as do other Caribbean writers.
48 Rudyard Kipling, a British writer of the high imperial period, is most remembered now for *Kim* (1901) and *The Jungle Book* (1894). For de Maupassant, see chapter 2, n. 2.
49 Angier, *Jean Rhys*, 419–22.
50 Rhys was a gifted translator but an intrusive one in the case of *Barred* in English. So there is good reason to see this story as Rhys's, even if it began as her husband's work. He did much the same thing himself (he translated *Voyage in the Dark* into Dutch) (Angier, *Jean Rhys*, 289). Like René in *Good Morning, Midnight*, the "Chevalier" is horrified by a woman who writes books, and talks, but "never feels anything" (*CS*:348).
51 Elaine Campbell and Pierrette Frickey titled their anthology of Caribbean women's writing *The Whistling Bird* (Boulder: Lynne Reinner and Kingston, Jamaica: Ian Randle, 1998).
52 Angier, *Jean Rhys*, 417.
53 See note 21, Hulme.
54 Cheryl Alexander Malcolm and David Malcolm, *Jean Rhys: A Study of the Short Fiction*, New York: Twayne, 1996; A. C. Morrell, "The World of Jean Rhys's Short

Stories," in ed. Pierrette Frickey, *Critical Perspectives on Jean Rhys*, Washington, DC: Three Continents Press, 1990, 95–102.

55 David Plante, *Difficult Women*, New York: Dutton, 1984.

56 Angier, *Jean Rhys*, 461.

Chapter 4 Reception

1 For early criticism, see Elgin W. Mellown, *Jean Rhys: A Descriptive and Annotated Bibliography of Works and Criticism*, New York: Garland Publishing, 1984, a source for many of the references below.

2 "Miss Rhys's Short Stories," *New York Times Book Review*, December 11, 1927, 28.

3 The review in *Nation and Athaneum*, 41 (June 25, 1929), 424, said that for Rhys to achieve "universal values" she needed to curtail her "emotionalism."

4 The *Times Literary Supplement* review thought her "subjective studies, written in the French manner in the first person" appeared in English "contrary" and "amateurish" (May 5, 1927, 320). D. B. Wyndham-Lewis, "Hinterland of Bohemia," *Saturday Review*, 143 (April 23, 1927), 637, thought Rhys's "balance" and "strict economy of the descriptive" made for this French effect.

5 The *New Statesman* found the characters "less than entertaining." Rhys had no "perception . . . of a beauty in life capable of dazzling her," though her style had "clarity and truthfulness," 31 (October 6, 1928, "Shorter Notices," 806). But in "Poignant Tragedy," *New York Times Book Review*, February 10, 1929, 8, Rhys's style is part of "the new tradition in prose, which shuns elaboration for sharpness and intensity of effect." For Robert Morss Lovett, *Bookman*, 69 (April 1929), 193, "Manner is perfectly adapted to matter." The *Times Literary Supplement* thought Marya's story "peculiarly sordid," October 4, 1928, 706. *The Saturday Review of Literature*, 5 (April 20, 1929), 936, compared her work favorably to Hemingway's *The Sun Also Rises*.

6 Gerald Gould's "New Novels. All Sorts of Societies," *Observer*, 7289 (February 8, 1931), 6, judges the emotional effect of the story to be "hard, dry, desperate" but sees the literary quality as "flawless." Others echoed reviews of *The Left Bank*: "a sordid little story. . .written with admirable clarity and economy of language . . . a waste of talent": *Times Literary Supplement*, 1518 (March 5, 1931), 180. American reviewers often liked the novel.

7 West's review is listed in Mellown, *Jean Rhys*, 24 as appearing in the London *Daily Telegraph*, but no further details are given.

8 Gladys Graham said *After Leaving Mr. Mackenzie* had "something of the balance and beauty of verse" ("A Bedraggled Career," *Saturday Review of Books*, 8 (July 25, 1931), 6.

9 Florence Haxton Britten, "Recent Leading Fiction," *New York Herald Tribune Books*, 11 (March 17, 1935), 10. Reviewers once more often preferred Rhys's style

to her themes. The *Times Literary Supplement*, November 1, 1934, 752, said that "Rhys's sense of beauty redeems much of the gloom and tragedy."

10 Cyril Connolly, "Three Shelves," *New Statesman*, 11 (January 4, 1936), 25–6.

11 "Lost Years," *Times Literary Supplement*, no. 1942 (April 22, 1939), 231. John Mair in "New Novels," *New Statesman*, 17 (April 22, 1939), thought the poetic style made the gigolo a tolerable character. Frank Swinnerton disliked the content but approved of the style ("New Novels. All Sorts," *Observer* 7717 [April 23, 1939], 6).

12 Kate O'Brien, "Fiction," *Spectator*, 162 (June 16, 1939), 1062.

13 "Jean Rhys: romancière inconnue," *Les nouvelles littéraires*, 880 (August 26, 1939), 8.

14 John Hampson, "Movements in the Underground," *Penguin New Writing*, 27, (April 1946), 133–51.

15 Alec Waugh, *The Sugar Islands: A Caribbean Travelogue*, New York: Farrar, Straus and Giroux, 1949, 278.

16 See Francis Wyndham, "An Inconvenient Novelist," *Tribune*, 721 (December 15, 1950), 16, 18; "Twenty-five years of the Novel," in ed. John Lehmann, *The Craft of Letters in England, A Symposium*, London: Cresset Press, 1956, 44–59; "Introduction," *Art and Literature*, 1 (March 1964), 173–7.

17 Gillian Hanscombe and Virginia L. Smyers, *Writing for Their Lives: The Modernist Women 1910–1940*, Boston: Northeastern University Press, 1987, 11.

18 Shari Benstock, *Women of the Left Bank: Paris, 1900–1940*, London: Virago Press, 1987.

19 Carole Angier, *Jean Rhys*, Boston, MA: Little, Brown, 1990, 178.

20 Thomas Staley *Jean Rhys: A Critical Study*, Austin: University of Texas Press, 1979.

21 Neville Braybrooke, "Between Dog and Wolf," *Spectator*, July 21, 1967, 77–8.

22 Elizabeth W. Frazer, *Library Journal*, 93 (May 1, 1968), 1919, called the reprint of *Voyage in the Dark* "marvelously contemporary." Carmen P. Collier, in *Best Sellers*, 28 (May 1, 1968), 58–9 said Rhys was ahead of her time, and that the novel would be better understood in the 1960s.

23 Walter Allen, "Bertha the Doomed," *New York Times Book Review*, June 18, 1967, 5.

24 John Thieme, "'Apparitions of Disaster': Brontëan Parallels in *Wide Sargasso Sea* and *Guerillas*," *Journal of Commonwealth Literature*, 14 (August 1979), 116–32.

25 David Cowart, *Literary Symbiosis: The Reconfigured Text in Twentieth Century Writing*, Athens, GA: University of Georgia Press, 1993.

26 Neville Braybrooke, "Jean Rhys," in ed. James Vinson, *Contemporary Novelists*, London: St. James Press, 1972, 1061–4. See also Neville Braybrooke, "The Return of Jean Rhys," *Caribbean Quarterly*, vol. 16, no. 4 (December 1970), 43–6.

27 Laurence Cole, "Jean Rhys," *Books and Bookmen*, 17 (January 1972), 20–1.

28 Elgin W. Mellown, "Character and Themes in the Novels of Jean Rhys," *Contemporary Literature*, 13 (1972), 458–75.

29 V. S. Naipaul, "Without a Dog's Chance," *New York Review of Books*, 18 (May 18, 1972), 29–31.

30 A. Alvarez, "The Best Living English Novelist," *New York Times Book Review*, March 17, 1974, 6–7.
31 John Hearne, "The Wide Sargasso Sea: A West Indian Reflection," *Cornhill Magazine*, 1080 (Summer 1974), 323–33.
32 Nancy J. Casey, "The 'Liberated' Woman in Jean Rhys's Later Short Fiction," *Revista Interamericana Review*, 4 (Summer 1974), 264–72.
33 Judith Thurman, "The Mistress and the Mask: Jean Rhys's Fiction," *MS*, 4 (January 1976), 50–2, 91.
34 Eunice de Souza, "Four Expatriate Writers," *Journal of the School of Languages* (Jawaharlal Nehru University), vol. 4, no. 2, (Winter 1976–7), 54–60.
35 Helen Tiffin, "Mirror and Mask: Colonial Motifs in the Novels of Jean Rhys," *World Literature Written in English*, 17 (April 1978), 328–41; Gayatri Spivak, "Three Women's Texts and a Critique of Imperialism," *Critical Inquiry*, vol. 12, no. 1, (Autumn 1985), 243–61. Recent claims that Rhys's *Voyage in the Dark* and other experimental writing in the late 1920s and early 1930s began to distance themselves from the "worship of form" and permit historical context are interesting if somewhat overstated.
36 See, for example, some aspects of Urmilla Seshagiri's interesting "Modernist Ashes, Postcolonial Phoenix," *Modernism/modernity*, vol. 13, no. 3, (2000), 487–505.
37 Todd K. Bender, "Jean Rhys and the Genius of Impressionism," *Studies in the Literary Imagination*, vol. 11, no. 2 (Fall 1978), 43–53.
38 Louis James, *Jean Rhys*, London: Longman, 1978.
39 Ibid., 13, 14.
40 Ibid., 13.
41 Staley, *Jean Rhys*, 6.
42 Peter Wolfe, *Jean Rhys*, Boston, MA: Twayne, 1980.
43 Arnold Davidson, *Jean Rhys*, New York: Frederick Ungar, 1985.
44 Ibid., 16.
45 Helen Nebeker, *Jean Rhys: Woman in Passage*, Montreal: Eden Press, 1981, 79.
46 Elizabeth Baer, "The Sisterhood of Jane Eyre and Antoinette Cosway," in ed. Elizabeth Abel *et al.*, *The Voyage In: Fictions of Female Development*, Hanover, NH: University Press of New England, 1983, 131–48.
47 See Nancy Harrison, *Jean Rhys and the Novel as Women's Text*: Chapel Hill: University of North Carolina Press, 1988, chapter 8, especially 196, 208.
48 Deborah Kelly Kloepfer, *The Unspeakable Mother: Forbidden Discourse in Jean Rhys and H.D.*, Ithaca, NY: Cornell University Press, 1989. Hilda Doolittle (1886–1961), born in Pennsylvania, knew Pound (and was almost engaged to him at one point) and Eliot. She wrote fiction as well as poetry, and was almost exactly a contemporary of Rhys.
49 Judith Kegan Gardiner, *Rhys, Stead, Lessing and the Politics of Empathy*, Bloomington: Indiana University Press, 1989; Molly Hite, *The Other Side of the Story: Structures and Strategies of Contemporary Feminist Narratives*: Ithaca, NY: Cornell University Press, 1989.

50 Wally Look Lai, "The Road to Thornfield Hall: An analysis of Jean Rhys's *Wide Sargasso Sea*," *New Beacon Reviews*, Collection 1, London: New Beacon Books, 1968, 38–52.
51 Kenneth Ramchand, *The West Indian Novel and Its Background*, London: Heineman (1970), 1983, chapter XIII, "Terrified Consciousness"; Fanon's phrase is attributed (p. 225).
52 Kamau Brathwaite, *Contradictory Omens*, Kingston, Jamaica: Savacou, 1974, 63, 34, 35.
53 Ibid., pp. 34–6.
54 Evelyn O'Callaghan, *"A Hot Place, Belonging to Us": Women Writing the West Indies* 1804–1939, New York: Routledge, 2004, 272n.
55 The exchange took place in more than one issue of the postcolonial journal, *Wasafiri*. See Peter Hulme, "The Place of *Wide Sargasso Sea*," *Wasafiri*, 20 (Autumn 1994), 5–11; Kamau Brathwaite, "A Post-Cautionary Tale of the Helen of Our Wars," *Wasafiri*, 22 (Autumn 1995), 69–81 (a reply to Hulme above); Peter Hulme, "A Response to Kamau Brathwaite," *Wasafiri*, 23 (Spring 1996), 49–50.
56 Maggie Humm, "Jean Rhys: Race, Gender and History, " in ed. Gina Wisker, *It's My Party: Reading Twentieth Century Women's Writing*, London: Pluto, 1994, 44–79; Jean d'Costa, "Jean Rhys, " in ed. Daryl Cumber Dance, *Fifty Caribbean Writers*, Westport: Greenwood Press, 1986, 390–404.
57 Veronica Gregg, *Jean Rhys's Historical Imagination: Reading and Writing the Creole*, Chapel Hill: University of North Carolina Press, 1995; Judith Raiskin, *Snow on the Canefields: Women's Writing and Creole Subjectivity*, Minneapolis: University of Minnesota Press, 1996.
58 Gregg, *Historical Imagination*, 37.
59 Raiskin, *Snow on the Canefields*, 110.
60 Karin Williamson, *Voyages in the Dark: Jean Rhys and Phyllis Shand Allfrey*, Warwick: University of Warwick Press, 1986.
61 Carolyn Vellenga Berman, *Creole Crossings: Domestic Fiction and the Reform of Colonial Slavery*, Ithaca, NY: Cornell University Press, 2006, chapter 6, pp. 169–86.
62 See Wilson Harris, "Carnival of Psyche: Jean Rhys's *Wide Sargasso Sea*," *Kunapipi*, vol. 2, no. 2 (1980), 142–50.
63 Peter Hulme, "The Locked Heart: The Creole Family Romance of *Wide Sargasso Sea* – A Historical and Biographical Analysis," *Jean Rhys Review*, vol. 6, no. 1, 20–35.
64 Mary Lou Emery, *Jean Rhys at "World's End": Novels of Colonial and Sexual Exile*, Austin: University of Texas Press, 1990; Moira Ferguson, *Colonialism and Gender Relations from Mary Wollstonecraft to Jamaica Kincaid: East Caribbean Connections*, New York: Columbia University Press, 1993.
65 Sue Thomas, *The Worlding of Jean Rhys*, Westport: Greenwood Press, 1999, 68–93, 158–67.
66 Carine M. Mardorossian, *Reclaiming the Difference: Caribbean Women Rewrite Postcolonialism*, Charlottesville: University of Virginia Press, 2005. Maryse

Condé's *Windward Heights* (trans. Richard Philcox, London: Faber and Faber, 1998), as Mardorossian points out, is dedicated respectfully to Emily Brontë, and does not "write back" in the manner of *Wide Sargasso Sea.*

67 Coral Ann Howells, *Jean Rhys*, New York: St Martin's Press, 1991.

68 Elaine Savory, *Jean Rhys*, Cambridge: Cambridge University Press, 1998, 2000, 2001, 2005. Chapter 9 and the Bibliography contain far more detail than is possible to include here.

69 Carol Dell' Amico's *Colonialism and the Modern Movement in the Early Novels of Jean Rhys*, New York: Routledge, 2005.

70 See, e.g., Pierrette Frickey, *Critical Perspectives on Jean Rhys*, Washington, DC: Three Continents Press 1990.

71 Ed. Carl Plasa, *Jean Rhys: Wide Sargasso Sea*, Houndmills: Palgrave Macmillan, 2001; ed. Judith L. Raiskin, *Wide Sargasso Sea*, New York: W.W. Norton, 1999.

72 Helen Carr, *Jean Rhys*, Plymouth: Northcote House, 1996.

73 The *Jean Rhys Review* has temporarily suspended publication.

74 Kristien Hemmerechts, *A Plausible Story and a Plausible Way of Telling It: A Structuralist Analysis of Jean Rhys's* Novels, Frankfurt: Peter Lang, 1987; Paula Le Gallez, *The Rhys Woman*, New York: St Martin's Press, 1990; Victoria Burrowes, *Whiteness and Trauma: The Mother–Daughter Knot in the Fiction of Jean Rhys, Jamaica Kincaid and Toni Morrison*, London: Palgrave, 2004.

75 Elgin W. Mellown, *Jean Rhys: A Descriptive and Annotated Bibliography of Works and Criticism*, New York: Garland Publishing, 1984; eds. Lisabeth Paravisini-Gebert and Olga Torres Seda, *Caribbean Women Novelists: An Annotated Bibliography*, Westport: Greenwood Press, 1993.

76 Alexis Lykiard, *Jean Rhys Revisited*, Exeter: Stride, 2000; and *Jean Rhys Afterward*, Nottingham: Shoestring, 2006.

77 "Jean Rhys" (anonymous author), in ed. Frank Magill, *Great Women Writers*, New York: Henry Holt and Company, 1994, 432–5.

78 Arnold Davidson, *Jean Rhys*, New York: Frederick Ungar, 1985; Sanford Sternlicht, *Jean Rhys*, New York: Twayne, 1997.

79 Sternlicht, *Jean Rhys*, 97.

80 Anne Simpson, *Territories of the Psyche: The Fiction of Jean Rhys*, New York: Palgrave, 2005.

81 Bianca Tarozzi, *La forma vincente: I romanzi di Jean Rhys*, Verona: Arsenale Editrice, 1984; Claire Joubert, *Lire de Feminine: Dorothy Richardson, Katherine Mansfield, Jean Rhys*, Paris: Messne, 1997; Corina Yoris-Villasana, *El Caribe tiene nombre de mujer: Indentitad cultural en la literature del Caribe anglofono: Jean Rhys*, Caracas: Universidad Catolica Andres Bello, 2004.

82 Lorna Sage, *Women in the House of Fiction: Post-War Women Novelists*, New York: Routledge, 1992, 47.

83 Ileana Rodriguez, *House/Garden/Nation: Space, Gender, Ethnicity in Post-Colonial Latin American Literatures by Women*, trans. Robert Carr and Illena Rodriguez, Durham, NC:Duke University Press, 1994.

84 Belinda Edmondson, *Making Men: Gender, Literary Authority and Women's Writing in Caribbean Narrative*, Durham, NC: Duke University Press, 1999, Margaret Paul Joseph, *Caliban in Exile: The Outsider in Caribbean Fiction*, New York: Greenwood Press, 1992; Leah Reade Rosenberg, *Nationalism and the Formation of Caribbean Literature*, New York: Palgrave Macmillan, 2007; Avril Horner and Sue Zlosnik, *Landscapes of Desire: Metaphors in Modern Women's Fiction*, New York: Harvester, 1990; Erica L. Johnson, *Home, Maison, Casa: The Politics of Location in Works by Jean Rhys, Marguerite Dumas, and Erminia Dell'Oro*, Madison: Farleigh Dickinson University Press, 2003.

85 Charles May, *The Short Story: The Reality of Artifice*, London: Routledge, 2002.

86 Stewart Brown, "Introduction," *The Oxford Book of Caribbean Short Stories*, Oxford: Oxford University Press, 1999, xxv.

87 Robert Antoni, *Blessed is the fruit*, New York: Henry Holt, 1997; Margaret Cezair-Thompson, *The True History of Paradise*, New York: Penguin Putman, 1999; Derek Walcott, "Jean Rhys," *Collected Poems 1948–1984*, New York: Farrar, Straus and Giroux, 1986, 427–9; Lorna Goodison, "Lullaby for Jean Rhys," *Selected Poems*, Ann Arbor: University of Michigan Press, 1992, 62; Olive Senior, "Meditation on Red," *Gardening in the Tropics*, Toronto: McClelland and Stewart, 1994, 44–53.

Select further reading

Carole Angier, *Jean Rhys*, Boston, MA: Little, Brown, 1990.

This biography is very helpful with regard to Rhys's life, especially her years in Britain, but should be read with caution as it conflates Rhys's fiction and her life to explain aspects of the latter which are difficult or impossible to accurately document.

Shari Benstock, *Women of the Left Bank: Paris, 1900–1940*, London: Virago Press, 1987.

A chapter on the 1930s in Paris contains a section on *Good Morning, Midnight*. The whole book provides an excellent context for understanding what it might have been like to be a woman writer in Paris in the first four decades of the twentieth century, before the Second World War broke out.

Carolyn Vellenga Berman, *Creole Crossings: Domestic Fiction and the Reform of Colonial Slavery*, Ithaca, NY: Cornell University Press, 2006.

Berman reads the role of the fictional representation of the Creole woman as key (and complex) with regard to the development of modern middle-class identity in slave-owning and slave-trading nations in the late eighteenth and early nineteenth centuries. She devotes a chapter to *Wide Sargasso Sea* because of its relation to *Jane Eyre*.

Kamau Brathwaite, *Contradictory Omens*, Kingston, Jamaica: Savacou, 1974

A crucial part of the early reception of Rhys as a Caribbean writer, which set off a controversy that still continues, this text should be historically contextualized.

Victoria Burrows, *Whiteness and Trauma: The Mother–Daughter Knot in the Fiction of Jean Rhys, Jamaica Kincaid and Toni Morrison*, London: Palgrave, 2004.

This reads Rhys through the lens of the psychology of mother–daughter connections, which excludes a great deal, whilst paying attention to an interesting element in Rhys's work.

Helen Carr, *Jean Rhys*, Plymouth: Northcote House, 1996.

A short but insightful and often original overview, as in its attention to the significance of Rhys's reference to Maupassant.

David Cowart, *Literary Symbiosis: The Reconfigured Text in Twentieth Century Writing*, Athens, GA: University of Georgia Press, 1993.

One chapter reads *Wide Sargasso Sea* along with *Jane Eyre*, marking the differences between the two.

Arnold Davidson, *Jean Rhys*, New York: Frederick Ungar, 1985.

An early critical study which affirms Rhys's technical skill and her innovative portrayals of women who flout society's conventions.

Belinda Edmondson, *Making Men: Gender, Literary Authority and Women's Writing in Caribbean Narrative*, Durham, NC: Duke University Press, 1999.

This includes some discussion of Rhys in the context of gender as a key element in the formation of canonical Caribbean texts.

Mary Lou Emery, *Jean Rhys at "World's End": Novels of Colonial and Sexual Exile*, Austin: University of Texas Press, 1990.

Emery provides meticulous and insightful readings of both Rhys's texts and contexts, arguing for a recognition of Rhys as writing between and across European and Caribbean modernisms, and providing a very valuable discussion of such aspects of her contemporary culture as the Paris Exhibition which figures in *Good Morning, Midnight*, and of her style, such as her employment of carnival motifs.

Moira Ferguson, *Colonialism and Gender Relations from Mary Wollstonecraft to Jamaica Kincaid: East Caribbean Connections*, New York: Columbia University Press, 1993.

This fascinating piece of literary history places Rhys in a dialogic relation with other women writers (British from the eighteenth and nineteenth centuries and Caribbean from the nineteenth and twentieth), whose work speaks to the intersections of British and Caribbean, slave and free, in the context of gender concerns.

Ed. Pierrette Frickey, *Critical Perspectives on Jean Rhys*, Washington, DC: Three Continents Press, 1990.

A very useful collection of reprinted early criticism on Rhys, along with autobiographical material and an extensive bibliography.

Judith Kegan Gardiner, *Rhys, Stead, Lessing and the Politics of Empathy*, Bloomington: Indiana University Press, 1989.

Gardiner carefully and thoughtfully tackles the thorny question of what constitutes women's writing via reading these three writers in relation to her concept of feminist empathy. Her chapter on Rhys's short stories and her discussion of *Wide Sargasso Sea* both recognize Rhys as outstanding.

Veronica Gregg, *Jean Rhys's Historical Imagination: Reading and Writing the Creole*, Chapel Hill: University of North Carolina Press, 1995.

Gregg's approach to Rhys is grounded in a close and careful reading of both her published work and her manuscripts and notebooks, and informed by major Caribbean historians and literary critics. This is an important counterbalance to critics who read her as European or modernist.

Wilson Harris, "Carnival of Psyche," in ed. Hena Maes-Jelinek, *Explorations*, Aarhus: Dangaroo, 1981, 125–33.

This essay not only marks praise of Rhys from a major Caribbean novelist but also deploys myth in reading *Wide Sargasso Sea* in ways that reflect Harris's own fictional practice and his location of Rhys within his reading of the Caribbean.

Nancy Harrison, *Jean Rhys and the Novel as Women's Text*, Chapel Hill: University of North Carolina Press, 1988.

This study contributes to feminist narrative theory (disclosing the political identities of female-authored texts) via a reading of *Voyage in the Dark* and *Wide Sargasso Sea*. Harrison references Freud, Derrida, Cixous and Lacan, though the majority of her book is a close reading of Rhys's work as writing back to a dominant masculinist culture.

Jeremy Hawthorn, *Multiple Personality and the Disintegration of Literary Character: From Oliver Goldsmith to Sylvia Plath*, London: Edward Arnold, 1983.

Hawthorn discusses Rhys with Faulkner, making a comparison of the plots and concerns with race of *Wide Sargasso Sea* and *Absalom, Absalom!*

Kristien Hemmerechts, *A Plausible Story and A Plausible Way of Telling It: A Structuralist Analysis of Jean Rhys's Novels*, Frankfurt: Peter Lang, 1987.

This lengthy study seems to be a barely revised dissertation and is distractingly absorbed in the strengths and weaknesses of structuralist theory. But it does ultimately realize the complexity of Rhys's narrative strategies.

Molly Hite, *The Other Side of the Story: Structures and Strategies of Contemporary Feminist Narratives*, Ithaca, NY: Cornell University Press, 1989.

Hite's book began from her interest in the absence of postmodern fiction by women and comes to redefine the relation of women's texts to postmodernism. Her chapter on Rhys pays close attention to Rhys's extraordinarily complex locations of male and female characters.

Avril Horner and Sue Zlosnik, *Landscapes of Desire: Metaphors in Modern Women's Fiction*, New York: Harvester, 1990.

This perspective on Rhys provides an interesting way into reading three of her texts and contextualizing her in relation to other women writers, including Wharton, Woolf and Atwood.

Coral Ann Howells, *Jean Rhys*, New York: St Martin's Press, 1991.

Though this short study predates recent developments in Rhys criticism, with that limitation it still remains one of the best introductory overviews of her work. Howells deftly located the three major strands of Rhys's writerly identity (woman, colonial, modernist) at a moment when this was urgently needed.

Peter Hulme, *Remnants of Conquest: The Island Caribs and Their Visitors, 1877–1998*, Oxford: Oxford University Press, 2000.

This widely researched and meticulous study of representations of the Carib people of the Caribbean includes a valuable detailed discussion of Rhys's direct and indirect references to the Caribs in her work.

Louis James, *Jean Rhys*, London: Longman, 1978.

This book appeared a year before Rhys's death and well before her papers were available. It takes 1894 mistakenly as her birthdate, but pays attention to Rhys's Caribbean origins and to the place of her work in relation to the Caribbean novel.

Erica L. Johnson, *Home, Maison, Casa: The Politics of Location in Works by Jean Rhys, Marguerite Dumas, and Erminia Dell'Oro*, Madison: Farleigh Dickinson University Press, 2003.

Centrally concerned with the results of exile and displacement and their contribution to the importance of representations of houses and homes in the work of three writers, Johnson juxtaposes the lack of an actual rooted home and writing as home.

Margaret Paul Joseph, *Caliban in Exile: The Outsider in Caribbean Fiction*, New York: Greenwood Press, 1992.

A reading of Rhys's Caribbean novels in the context of Shakespeare's characters Prospero and Caliban, which have become iconic in Caribbean literary discourse.

Deborah Kelly Kloepfer, *The Unspeakable Mother: Forbidden Discourse in Jean Rhys and H.D.*, Ithaca, NY: Cornell University Press, 1989.

This is interesting not only for its comparison of H.D. and Rhys but for Kloepfer's high feminist interest in the "absent mother" as an informing motif in their work. Her argument is located in the moment when American and French feminist theory were opposed. Kloepfer's study is strongly informed by Julia Kristeva's work.

Paula Le Gallez, *The Rhys Woman*, New York: St Martin's Press, 1990.

This title illuminates the debate in early Rhys criticism over whether or not her characters were in fact all the same woman at different stages and ages. Le Gallez reads Rhys's texts closely for their narrative structures: she also speculated about Rhys's "unconscious feminism" and resisted feminist readings of Rhys.

Cheryl Alexander Malcolm and David Malcolm, *Jean Rhys: A Study of the Short Fiction*, New York: Twayne, 1996.

This is a compilation of the Malcolms' critical discussion of Rhys's stories, biographical material (letters and conversations with David Plante), and extracts from reviews and essays on the stories, providing a basic introduction and useful resource.

Carine M. Mardorossian, *Reclaiming the Difference: Caribbean Women Rewrite Postcolonialism*, Charlottesville: University of Virginia Press, 2005.

This New World-centered study argues that a new phase of postcolonial discourse has been created by Caribbean women writers, including Rhys, which transcends old divisions and boundaries and, by the inclusion of Spanish, French and English-language texts, affiliates with the development of comparative Caribbean literary studies.

Sylvie Maurel, *Jean Rhys*, New York: St Martin's Press, 1998.

In this close reading of Rhys's texts, Maurel argues that Rhys's idea of the feminine is deconstructive, employing irony, parody and intertextuality.

Elgin W. Mellown, *Jean Rhys: A Descriptive and Annotated Bibliography of Works and Criticism*, New York: Garland Publishing, 1984.

In its detailed account of early reviews and criticism, an invaluable resource for Rhys scholars.

Helen Nebeker, *Jean Rhys: Woman in Passage*, Montreal: Eden Press, 1981.

An eccentric reading of Rhys, heavily informed by Eurocentric feminist mythology and ignoring the Caribbean. This is however the first female-authored study of Rhys, and marks the claim on her by late twentieth-century European feminism.

Teresa O'Connor, *Jean Rhys: The West Indian Novels*, New York: New York University Press, 1986.

An insightful and well-informed reading of *Voyage in the Dark* and *Wide Sargasso Sea*, linking Rhys's colonial experience and the theme of gender, and including close reference to Rhys's notebooks, letters, manuscripts and autobiography as evidence of the process of making fiction out of life experience.

Eds. Lisabeth Paravisini-Gebert and Olga Torres Seda, *Caribbean Women Novelists: An Annotated Bibliography*, Westport: Greenwood Press, 1993.

A useful resource, especially with regard to critical summaries of essays on Rhys that can be hard to locate, but it has errors (Rhys's birthdate is given as 1894, Mr. Ramage is "Mr. Rampage" in the title of one of her stories, Ford Madox Ford is Ford Maddox Ford and Prospero is Prosper).

Ed. Carl Plasa, *Jean Rhys: Wide Sargasso Sea*, Houndmills: Palgrave Macmillan, 2001.

This reader's guide to essential criticism on this novel provides an extremely useful resource, divided into chapters which each focus on either a chronological period or a thematic critical approach (such as race or a concern with history).

Judith Raiskin, *Snow on the Canefields: Women's Writing and Creole Subjectivity*, Minneapolis: University of Minnesota Press, 1996.

Raiskin locates Rhys in a line of women writers she identifies as British-connected Creoles (Olive Schreiner, Jean Rhys, Michelle Cliff and Zoe Wicomb, two from the Caribbean and two from South Africa, two clearly white and two of mixed-race origin). All these writers complicate racial and cultural categories.

Ed. Judith L. Raiskin, *Wide Sargasso Sea*, New York: W. W. Norton, 1999.

This edition contains a helpful introduction to criticism on *Wide Sargasso Sea* through a group of essays and a bibliography.

Kenneth Ramchand, *The West Indian Novel and Its Background*, London: Heineman (1970), 1983.

This pioneering, well-researched history of the early West Indian novel located Rhys's *Wide Sargasso Sea* in relation to "terrified consciousness" in white Creoles at and after Emancipation, and so drew resistance from the poet and historian Kamau Brathwaite.

Ileana Rodriguez, *House/Garden/Nation: Space, Gender, Ethnicity in Post-Colonial Latin American Literatures by Women*, trans Robert Carr and Ileana Rodriguez, Durham, NC: Duke University Press, 1994.

The chapter on Rhys here claims her as within Latin American literary space (that is, Caribbean space), and foregrounds nature (cultivated or wild) and the island as nation.

Caroline Rody, *The Daughter's Return: African-American and Caribbean Women's Fictions of History*, Oxford: Oxford University Press, 2001.

This devotes one section to reading *Wide Sargasso Sea* in the context of a study of representations of black daughters seeking lost black mothers (*Wide Sargasso Sea* offers a study in the relation of a black mother/white daughter in Christophine and Antoinette).

Leah Reade Rosenberg, *Nationalism and the Formation of Caribbean Literature*, New York: Palgrave Macmillan, 2007.

Rosenberg successfully argues the importance of Caribbean literary history before the 1950s, and reads Rhys in relation to it, marking her use of the "colonial romance," modernist visual art and newspapers in her fiction.

Lorna Sage, *Women in the House of Fiction: Post-War Women Novelists*, New York: Routledge, 1992.

This lively book usefully contextualizes Rhys: the chapter in which her work is discussed, titled "Displaced Persons," also includes the Australian Christina Stead, the Canadian Elizabeth Smart, the American Tillie Olsen and the French Françoise Sagan.

Elaine Savory, *Jean Rhys*, Cambridge: Cambridge University Press, 1998, 2000, 2001, 2005.

A title in the Cambridge series on African and Caribbean writers, this seeks to locate Rhys's entire work as deeply informed by the Caribbean aesthetically as well as thematically. Longer than this present study, it includes chapters on Rhys's novels and stories, Rhys's life and contexts and Rhys criticism.

Anne B. Simpson, *Territories of the Psyche: the Fiction of Jean Rhys*, New York: Palgrave, 2005.

This follows earlier studies based in psychology and psychoanalysis, and like them is a particularly partial reading, using Rhys's work as a kind of series of case studies.

Thomas Staley, *Jean Rhys: A Critical Study*, Austin: University of Texas Press, 1979.

An early overview study of Rhys which foregrounds her life (but takes 1894 as her birthdate). Staley recognized her extraordinary achievement and her unique style.

Sanford Sternlicht, *Jean Rhys*, New York: Twayne, 1997.

This is an introductory overview of Rhys's work and life, including a helpful chronology and an annotated bibliography. It is however often reductive in its readings of Rhys texts and does not provide a sense of the development of Rhys studies.

John Thieme, *Postcolonial Con-Texts: Writing Back to the Canon*, London: Continuum, 2001.

The chapter of this study of intertextuality which centrally focuses on *Wide Sargasso Sea* and *Jane Eyre* also discusses other texts by Caribbean and Canadian authors that reference the Bronte sisters.

Sue Thomas, *The Worlding of Jean Rhys*, Westport: Greenwood Press, 1999.

A deeply scholarly discussion of Rhys's work from a new historicist perspective. It offers a great deal of information on cultural elements in Rhys's work (which is defined as intertextual), from Dominican journalism and the role of obeah in the collective imaginary of Dominica in Rhys's childhood to anxieties in England about "amateur" prostitution.

Peter Wolfe, *Jean Rhys*, Boston: Twayne, 1980.
An early overview, which accepts the now discredited idea that Rhys's protagonists are all the same woman at different stages of life, reiterates the mistaken 1894 birthdate and includes a good deal of plot summary.

Index

Cambridge Introductions to . . .

AUTHORS

Jane Austen Janet Todd
Samuel Beckett Ronan McDonald
Walter Benjamin David Ferris
J. M. Coetzee Dominic Head
Joseph Conrad John Peters
Jacques Derrida Leslie Hill
Emily Dickinson Wendy Martin
George Eliot Nancy Henry
T. S. Eliot John Xiros Cooper
William Faulkner Theresa M. Towner
F. Scott Fitzgerald Kirk Curnutt
Michel Foucault Lisa Downing
Robert Frost Robert Faggen
Nathaniel Hawthorne Leland S. Person
Zora Neale Hurston Lovalerie King
James Joyce Eric Bulson
Herman Melville Kevin J. Hayes
Sylvia Plath Jo Gill
Edgar Allen Poe Benjamin F. Fisher
Ezra Pound Ira Nadel
Jean Rhys Elaine Savory
Shakespeare Emma Smith
Shakespeare's Comedies Penny Gay
Shakespeare's History Plays Warren Chernaik
Shakespeare's Tragedies Janette Dillon
Harriet Beecher Stowe Sarah Robbins
Mark Twain Peter Messent
Virginia Woolf Jane Goldman
W. B. Yeats David Holdeman
Edith Wharton Pamela Knights
Walt Whitman M. Jimmie Killingsworth

TOPICS

The American Short Story Martin Scofield
Creative Writing David Morley
Early English Theatre Janette Dillon
English Theatre, 1660–1900 Peter Thomson
Francophone Literature Patrick Corcoran
Modernism Pericles Lewis
Modern Irish Poetry Justin Quinn
Narrative (second edition) H. Porter Abbott
The Nineteenth-Century American Novel Gregg Crane
Postcolonial Literatures C. L. Innes
Russian Literature Caryl Emerson
The Short Story in English Adrian Hunter
Theatre Historiography Thomas Postlewait
Theatre Studies Christopher Balme
Tragedy Jennifer Wallace